The Recurrence of
the End Times

POLITICAL THEORY FOR TODAY

Series Editor: Richard Avramenko, University of Wisconsin, Madison

Political Theory for Today seeks to bring the history of political thought out of the jargon-filled world of the academy into the everyday world of social and political life. The series brings the wisdom of texts and the tradition of political philosophy to bear on salient issues of our time, especially issues pertaining to human freedom and responsibility, the relationship between individuals and the state, the moral implications of public policy, health and human flourishing, public and private virtues, and more. Great thinkers of the past have thought deeply about the human condition and their situations—books in Political Theory for Today build on that insight.

Titles Published

The Recurrence of the End Times: Voegelin, Hegel, and the Stop-History Movements by Michael J. Colebrook

Willmoore Kendall: Tribune and Teacher of the American People by Christopher Owen

The Politics of Private Property: Contested Claims to Ownership in U.S. Cultural Discourse by Simone Knewitz

The Political Philosophy of the European City: From Polis, through City-State, to Megalopolis by Ferenc Hörcher

John Locke and the Uncivilized Society: Resistance and Individualism in America Today, by Scott Robinson

Welcoming the Other: Student, Stranger, and Divine edited by N. Susan Laehn and Thomas R. Laehn

Cosmopolitanism and its Discontents: Rethinking Politics in the Age of Brexit and Trump, edited by Lee Ward

Eric Voegelin's Asian Political Thought edited by Lee Trepanier

The Spartan Drama of Plato's Laws by Eli Friedland

Idolizing the Idea: A Critical History of Modern Philosophy by Wayne Cristaudo

Eric Voegelin Today: Voegelin's Political Thought in the 21st Century, edited by Scott Robinson, Lee Trepanier, David Whitney

The Recurrence of the End Times

Voegelin, Hegel, and the Stop-History Movements

Michael J. Colebrook

LEXINGTON BOOKS
Lanham • Boulder • New York • London

Published by Lexington Books
An imprint of The Rowman & Littlefield Publishing Group, Inc.
4501 Forbes Boulevard, Suite 200, Lanham, Maryland 20706
www.rowman.com

86-90 Paul Street, London EC2A 4NE

British Library Cataloguing in Publication Information Available

Library of Congress Cataloging-in-Publication Data

Names: Colebrook, Michael J., 1988- author.
 Title: The recurrence of the end times : Voegelin, Hegel, and the
  stop-history movements / Michael J. Colebrook.
 Description: Lanham : Lexington Books, [2022] | Series: Political theory
  for today | Includes bibliographical references and index. | Summary:
  "The Recurrence of the End Times: Voegelin, Hegel, and the Stop-History
  Movements explores the deep connection between modern political
  ideologies and the secular eschatological hopes and dreams of a
  post-Christian society"-- Provided by publisher.
 Identifiers: LCCN 2021970002 (print) | LCCN 2021970093 (ebook) | ISBN
  9781793651341 (cloth) | ISBN 9781793651365 (pbk) | ISBN
  9781793651358 (epub)
 Subjects: LCSH: Voegelin, Eric, 1901-1985. | Hegel, Georg Wilhelm
  Friedrich, 1770-1831. | History--Philosophy. | Political
  science--Philosophy. | History--Religious aspects--Christianity. |
  Christianity and politics. | Eschatology. | Ideology.
 Classification: LCC D16.9 .C593 2022 (print) | LCC D16.9 (ebook) | DDC
  901--dc23/eng/20220204
 LC record available at https://lccn.loc.gov/2021970002
 LC ebook record available at https://lccn.loc.gov/2021970093

To my wife, the divine "Parousia" in my life . . .

Contents

Introduction

What could two European political philosophers possibly offer American policy-makers living in the twenty-first century? Their books and theories have begun to accumulate dust generations old—in Voegelin's case, four to six decades; in Hegel's, close to two centuries—read exclusively perhaps by political historians, but of seemingly little relevance to those bearing the weight of policy formation. What is more, how relevant to our contemporary world is a scholarly exploration of the *relationship* between these two thinkers, considering how abstruse and specific the topic? It seems an endeavor best left to the cloistered curiosity of academia.

My answer to these justifiable queries is rather blunt: we can learn a great deal. For better or for worse, the world we inhabit is in fundamental ways Hegel's world. Wherever we turn on the great globe, we see the impact of his thought. Communist regimes and movements—illegitimate Hegelian offspring—still persist as full-fledged political entities in dozens of countries, including several powerful ones. Fascistic systems—another Hegelian progeny—exist in still others. Indeed, the modern Nation-State itself, even in its healthiest manifestations, bears the mark of Hegel's thought. Hegel was, after all, the greatest theorist of the State. We live in a Hegelian age precisely because we live in the Modern Age. Modernity is Hegelian.

Voegelin is also important for the very same reasons. If the world we dwell in is Modern and Hegelian, it helps to know precisely why this is significant. Few other theorists have spent so much time trying to diagnose the particular ailments of the Hegelian age and have offered tentative paths forward in navigating it. At a crucially deep level, Voegelin helps us to see the Modern Age for what it is, and frees us to analyze it without succumbing to its most pervasive and dangerous derailments. One of the most destabilizing of these elements is the abiding presence of secularized eschatological thinking in the political arena and, in some cases, in the foreign policy realm. The metastatic faith that would transform the political world into an earthly paradise remains active in numerous ways. In more or less explicit forms, the "end of history" appears just around the corner to those naïve or psychologically disturbed enough to embrace it. Political saviors and Messiahs—those we hope will

1

carry out this desired change—exist in abundance. Perfect equality, the end of war, complete freedom from reliance on fossil fuels, Sharia law—pick your "cause"; Voegelin helps us to analyze them and immunizes us against their extremist variants.

It is true: Voegelin misreads Hegel, as do so many people. So why make a topic of one theorist's misunderstanding of another theorist? Because Voegelin, like so many others, misreads Hegel in important ways. Indeed, speaking generally, it is not an exaggeration to say that misreadings of Hegel have had a more profound impact on the unfolding of history in the twentieth and twenty-first centuries than any other factor. But unlike the vast majority of Hegel misreadings, which have caused an unspeakable amount of death and suffering, Voegelin misreads Hegel in a way that helps to restore order on an individual and societal level.

The topic of this study is therefore Voegelin's misreading of Hegel. While I am certainly not the first to cover this subject, I am the first to do it in a comprehensive full-length study. All other accounts have been incredibly insightful, but partial and incomplete. I aim to bring together all elements of this relationship, including the most crucial piece yet: an account of *why* Voegelin gets Hegel wrong. This theoretical relationship stands at the intersection of psychology, history, foreign policy, politics, and theology. Its tensions, misunderstandings, and ambiguities reveal a treasure trove of insight into our current political predicament. Its importance cannot be overstated.

PART I

General Introduction to the End of History Controversy

Chapter 1

The End of History, Identity Politics, and Transcendence

Alexandre Kojève is one of Hegel's most widely read commentators in the Western world, and his influence in the twentieth and twenty-first centuries was immense. Behind the scenes, he gave voice to what would become the theoretical presuppositions of countless Western politicians, citizens, and intellectuals. Neoconservatives, Progressives, and Democratic Peace Theorists, among others, bear his impression. However, most who use his ideas for policy rarely know of their theoretical basis.

In recent decades, we have seen several published books speculating on the ideas Kojève espoused, the most important of which is the idea that history—understood as a teleological development with a beginning and end—has reached its culminating point in the modern liberal democratic State. According to this theory, all that remains for global societies to do is fully conform to this irrefutable political, moral, and social standard. Self-consciously continuing the legacy of Kojève, Francis Fukuyama—the most articulate and influential End of History speculator, who originally published his *The End of History and the Last Man* in 1992—makes the case that the fall of the Berlin Wall in 1989 and the unprecedented increase in democratic revolutions worldwide marked the end of Mankind's ideological evolution. His argument was not that wars and political catastrophes will somehow cease or that all political struggles will end. Instead, he claimed there was an *emerging* "global consensus" that liberal democracy is the only viable and legitimate form of government and that only it is fully equipped to face the tough environmental and economic challenges of the coming centuries. He suggests that while earlier forms of government were characterized by "grave defects" and "irrationalities" that led to their eventual collapse, liberal democracy, if understood correctly, is fundamentally free from such self-undermining contradictions.

Of course, at first glance, his argument appears empirically overstated. While the jury is still out on the long-term endurance of the Chinese Communist Party or the Russian Federation, as of this writing, the power and influence of these very undemocratic regimes only seem to be growing, with no end in sight.[1] In the policy world, there are also two other competing theoretical visions of the future course of history that seem convincing: Samuel Huntington's *The Clash of Civilizations and the Remaking of World Order* and John Mearsheimer's *The Tragedy of Great Power Politics*.[2] These latter works explicitly critique Fukuyama's thesis and provide reasonable alternatives to his Kojèvian historical vision. What is more, we could also point to the very severe problems that plague the Western world: the imminent ecological collapse, widespread poverty and income disparity, inflation, and an increasing budget deficit. These are real problems and contradictions that affect real people.

Yet, for our purposes, these objections would miss the true heart of the issue, since Fukuyama claims that the problems facing the modern democratic world are simply failures of these societies to fully live up to the standards and ideals—namely liberty and equality—which liberal democracy has set up for itself. Though some contemporary societies may fail to achieve stable liberal democratic governments, and others might lapse back into more primitive and irrational forms of rule like theocracy or military dictatorship, Fukuyama argues that the *ideal* of liberal democracy cannot be improved upon.

His argument is based upon two fundamental premises: the first is that the foundations of the modern scientific method, once adopted by a society, cannot simply be put aside when its consequences become hard to swallow. This is a good starting point, according to Fukuyama, because modern science is the only important social activity that by "common consensus" is both cumulative and directional, even if its ultimate impact on human happiness is ambiguous.[3] No matter what one's religious, ethnic, or national background, everyone can agree on scientific results and methodologies. Modern natural science has therefore had a uniform effect on all societies that have experienced it. One can be Russian, Chinese, Muslim, Catholic, or Atheist; the conclusions of this science will be universal, and the technologies to which it gives rise, which gradually submit nature to the will of humans, provide for the satisfaction of *universal* wants and desires. This same technology confers *decisive military advantages* on those countries that possess it. Given the continuing possibility of war in the international system of states, no state that values its independence can ignore the need for defensive modernization. Technology also makes possible a "limitless" accumulation of wealth and the ongoing satisfaction of an ever-expanding set of human desires. Fukuyama continues:

This process guarantees an increasing homogenization of all human societies, regardless of their historical origins or cultural inheritances. All countries undergoing economic modernization must increasingly resemble one another: they must unify nationally on the basis of a centralized state, urbanize, replace traditional forms of social organization like tribe, sect, and family with economically rational forms of social organization based on function and efficiency, and provide for the universal education of their citizens. Such societies have become increasingly linked with one another through global markets and the spread of a universal consumer culture. Moreover, the logic of modern natural science would seem to dictate a universal evolution in the direction of capitalism.[4]

These insights are the basis for what has come to be known as Democratic Modernization Theory, which has powerful adherents in the policy world.[5] Nonetheless, as Fukuyama admits, this purely *economic* interpretation of a "universal history" only goes so far. While it is true that, for him, an analysis of the mechanisms of globalization shows us a remarkable trend toward societies becoming increasingly technology/consumer-oriented and capitalistic, this trend alone does not prove his thesis that democracy is the only legitimate form of government. One only has to point to the numerous "successful" authoritarian capitalist regimes, such as present-day China, Singapore, and Thailand, to demonstrate that a link may not exist between consumer-oriented capitalism and democratic political structures.

This gap brings Fukuyama to the second major premise of his work: that only what he calls "universal recognition" can satisfy human nature, and that this "universal recognition" can only be provided by a legitimate liberal democracy.[6] Drawing on insights from Kojève's lectures on Hegel's *Phenomenology of Spirit*, he asserts that there is something in human nature—Plato called it *Thymos*, Hobbes called it pride, Rousseau called it *amour-propre*—that is not satisfied with mere biological subsistence or even being a "consumer" whose *every* appetite could be satiated. Human beings value themselves; they have a certain amount of dignity or self-esteem, which they crave for others to recognize. The purely "economic" understanding of historical development overlooks this aspect of human nature. If human beings could be fully satisfied with the bare necessities of life—and these even in surplus—then it might be true that there is no direct causal link between capitalism and democracy. Societies would simply develop toward whatever particular political regime, given its concrete circumstances, could most efficiently produce economic prosperity. As we see in present-day China, State-run forms of capitalism are just as, if not more, efficient at creating wealth than their more liberal counterparts.

Importantly, if Fukuyama wanted to make the case that there is a necessary historical movement toward *both* capitalism and liberal democracy, he would have to make his arguments in light of a coherent philosophical anthropology that makes this development necessary. As he comments,

> Any attempt to portray the basic human impulse driving the liberal democratic revolutions of the late twentieth century, or indeed of any liberal revolution since those of America and France in the eighteenth century, as merely an economic one, would be radically incomplete. The mechanism created by modern natural science remains a partial and ultimately unsatisfying account of the historical process. Free government exercises a positive pull of its own: When the President of the United States or the President of France praises liberty and democracy, they are praised as good things in themselves, and this praise seems to have resonance for people around the world.[7]

In sum, the most fundamental reason why liberal democratic governments are more legitimate and will always have an undeniable appeal is that they alone can "recognize" each particular citizen—that is, *they can endow each of them with inherent rights and treat them equally before the law*. Whereas fascist or communist dictatorships must repress civil society—the realm of individual ambition, self-expression, and self-assertion—in favor of some national or "moral" cause, liberal democracy allows its citizens to determine themselves according to their unique personalities and life-style choices. In the long term, the oversight of this fundamental desire in human nature all but guarantees the fall of undemocratic governments.

As already mentioned, this theory is not without its critics. In *Living in the End Times*, Slavoj Zizek has harshly denounced the liberal democratic triumphalism implicit in the thesis of the *End of History*, criticizing its supporters as blatant ideological dreamers who are all the worse for seeing themselves as being postideological. In this view, the idea that there is a "global consensus" that liberal democracy is the only legitimate form of government and that the foreign policy of these supposedly enlightened and peaceful governments should be aimed at "modernizing" the globe is an illusion, a mask concealing its own particularity which it imposes on others as universal. This amounts to no less than a *liberal democratic imperialism*, which masks its true horrors from domestic populations by manipulating linguistic symbols used in marketing schemes and political propaganda. "Today," as Zizek argues, "this fundamental level of constitutive ideology assumes the guise of its very opposite: non-ideology."[8] What makes the hegemony of Western liberal democratic societies so dangerous is their intransigent self-perception as societies *beyond* all of the ideological warfare of previous generations. Not only is this self-designation empirically hypocritical—something which can be seen in the horrible conditions in the nations of the developing/undeveloped world, which Western governments and multinational corporations have exploited and prevented from self-determination—but it also functions as an ideological *blinding mechanism* that succeeds in covering over the violent real-world consequences of this ideological imperialism. For Zizek, the liberal democratic critique of old-world ideologies—that they impose some sort of "tyranny of the good"—is incredibly deceptive: the more this program begins to permeate society, the more it begins to turn into what it originally criticized. Even worse, it now has a good conscience on its side. The claim by these same liberal democratic societies to want nothing but the lesser evil—in Churchill's famous words, "the worst form of government, except for all the rest"—gradually replicates the features of the enemy. In other words, the apparent postideological anti-utopianism of liberal democratic societies has gradually morphed into a *new brand* of ideology and utopianism. For Zizek, the global liberal order clearly presents itself as the best of all possible worlds; its modest rejection of utopias ends with the imposition of its own market-liberal utopia that will supposedly become reality when we subject ourselves entirely to the mechanisms of the market and universal human rights, leaving behind all of the "irrationalities" of more traditional societies. Further, these societies naively believe they can perpetuate themselves *ad infinitum* with unlimited prosperity and an endless progress toward an increasingly high standard of living. This, for Zizek, is a myth and the ultimate tragedy of the capitalist/liberal democratic order. Behind this dream of the end of History "lurks the ultimate Totalitarian nightmare."[9]

Despite the pathos, incisiveness, and energy of Zizek's critiques, they do not really touch the more subtle argument made throughout Fukuyama's book. Fukuyama's argument is *not* that the current hegemonic liberal democratic regimes are completely free from ideology, oppression, and poverty, or that their foreign policies have not at certain points led to antidemocratic or exploitative results. Rather, as I emphasized earlier, it is that the *ideal* of liberal democracy, as well as its concomitant focus on liberty and equality, cannot be surpassed. *Fukuyama is talking about a consensus of the ideal, not the real.* The failures of concrete societies to actualize or promote these goals do not at all call into question the desirability of the goals themselves. We can see this desirability clearly in the disingenuous appeal to democratic principles even among the most ruthless dictators. The cases in which supposedly liberal democratic regimes have taken measures to promote their own interests at the expense of the oppressed and marginalized of their own domestic populations or of those abroad are simply examples of concretely existent democratic governments failing to live up to the standards to which they pay lip service. One could even say that Zizek, in his justified indignation at the actions of Western governments and multinational corporations, is voicing his opposition in the name of the same ideals that these societies sometimes hypocritically praise. His assertion that the self-perceived postideological mind-set is in reality the worst form of ideology, therefore, does not touch Fukuyama himself, but only his disowned intellectual progeny, the neocon-servatives, of whom he has now washed his hands.

My defense of Fukuyama should not be misunderstood. His book on the *End of History* is genuinely an unsurpassed attempt to make sense of interna-tional relations in the 1990s and beyond. Yet, as our penetration of Voegelin's work will later show us, it is not without its defects and shortcomings, something that Fukuyama has himself acknowledged since the time of its publication in 1992.[10] For our analysis, it is important that Fukuyama's book is representative of particular strands of American self-understanding and Grand Strategy in global affairs. This much is widely accepted. What is not as well known is that Fukuyama situates himself within the same tradition of speculation on a "universal history" as Kojève and, more importantly, Hegel. Accordingly, if Eric Voegelin provides a convincing critique of the principles underlying this "universal history," Francis Fukuyama's, which relies almost entirely on it, would also fall. Voegelin's critique could thus have extremely far-reaching implications for American self-understanding and American foreign policy.

While it is undoubtedly true that Fukuyama eventually expressed res-ervations about his thesis and also gradually distanced himself from the Neoconservative movement to which he helped give rise, he still, in more recent writings, retains the Kojèvian philosophical anthropology expressed in the *End of History*.[11] Here, man's most primordial and basic desire is for universal recognition.[12] A quick look at his response to a common objection to his thesis is illustrative of this point. Critics often claim that the Islamic world is inimical to the development of viable liberal democracies.[13] Especially since the September 11 World Trade Center attacks, many people have come to see Islam as not only anti-American but also antidemocratic. Fukuyama acknowledges that this criticism is not entirely without legitimacy. There is no question that, looking around the world, one sees a broad Muslim exception to the overall pattern of democratic development elsewhere. People assume that there must be something inherent to Islamic doctrine, such as the unity of Church and State, which acts as a cultural barrier to this development.

Still, Fukuyama suggests that it is doubtful the resistance to liberal democ-racy stems from the nature of Islam itself. Instead, there may be some sort of "cultural delay," he claims. Islam merely needs to catch up, and this it can only do by going through the same political struggles that the West itself had to go through hundreds of years earlier. He points his readers to Western development: it is evident that Christianity was used at one time to support hierarchy, oppression, and slavery. Now, in contemporary societies, we see it as supportive of liberal democracy. Because religious doctrines are subject to constantly renewed political interpretations, it would not be too implausible to believe that Islam will undergo a similar development to Christianity in the West. In fact, there have already been many relatively successful democracies with predominantly Muslim populations, such as Indonesia and Turkey. If one is to describe the political landscape accurately, one would have to recognize that the resistance to liberal democracy does not seem to come from Islam, but rather from predominantly *Arab* countries. This trend, Fukuyama remarks, probably has more to do with a "survival of tribalism" than Islam itself.[14]

Another reason why this resistance to democracy has very little to do with Islam *per se* is that the radical Islamism of Al Qaida, ISIS, and the like should be understood, not as natural offshoots of Islam, but as *political ideology*. Fukuyama comments,

> The writings of Said Qutb, the founder of the Muslim Brotherhood in Egypt, or Osama Bin Laden and his ideologues within Al Qaeda, make use of political ideas about the state, revolution, and the aestheticization of violence that do not come out of any genuine Islamic tradition but out of the radical ideologies of Left and Right—that is to say, of Fascism and Communism—from twentieth century Europe. These doctrines, which are extremely dangerous, do not reflect any core teachings of Islam, but make use of Islam for political purposes. They have become popular in many Arab countries and among Muslims in Europe because of the deep alienation that exists in these communities. Radical Islamism is thus not the reassertion of some traditional Islamic cultural practice, but should be seen in the context of modern identity politics. It emerges precisely when traditional cultural identities are disrupted by modernization and a pluralistic democratic order that creates a disjuncture between one's inner self and external social practice.[15]

This last comment is very peculiar. Whether or not the various anti-Western terrorist organizations have anything to do with "genuine Islam" is a question I will not go into here. Instead, what interests me is Fukuyama's disguised concession to his objectors. The main emphasis of his argument in this passage is that radical Islamism is a reaction, whether religious or political, to the *disruption* modernization and pluralistic democratic orders cause in the individual psyche. This disruption is entirely on the level of what he is here calling "identity politics." Is this an admission that liberal democracy is not, will not be, and cannot be, completely satisfying to individuals and cultural groups?[16] Does this not undermine the entire argument of the *End of History*, that there is a "global consensus" that liberal democracy is the ideological victor in the global community? These examples show that, from the beginning, liberal democracy has only succeeded in creating, to put it in Hegelian language, antitheses and contradictions to itself. The "recognition" provided by these societies is not recognized in its turn. Adherents of identity politics demand something the political order cannot give. So, the thymotic energies of the various identities are unleashed, acting as a consistently subversive element in modern societies.

Fukuyama concedes this point by acknowledging that the historical process is more "open" than he initially thought. Yet, might it perhaps be possible that his reasons for conceding defeat are still based upon a restricted theoretical horizon? Has he maybe failed to develop an adequate philosophical anthropology that would enable him fully to comprehend his insights into the open-ended character of the historical process? Perhaps it is possible that *both* Fukuyama's original thesis—that history had come to its end in liberal democracy—and his reasons for recognizing its limitations—because liberal democracy is not fully satisfying to some cultures and individuals—are grounded in *the same theoretical mistake*, having its roots in the Kojèvian philosophical anthropology. Both his original thesis and his later qualification of it assume "identity politics" is the most important thing for understanding political order. In this view, the desire to have one's "identity" recognized is the central political problem.

This is precisely where I believe Voegelin provides a much-needed corrective to Fukuyama's Kojèvian premises. Voegelin's political philosophy fully deserves to find its proper place in contemporary political discourse, which has become saturated with theoretically inadequate tools for understanding our contemporary world, for just this reason. Unless we have an adequate philosophical anthropology, there is no way to orient ourselves in the contemporary political scene. Fukuyama is the paradigmatic case. Men simply desire recognition, according to him. They want their unique personalities and identities acknowledged and affirmed, whether this is a religious identity, secular identity, sexual orientation, and so forth. This recognition can only be provided in the universal homogenous state, according to the argument in the *End of History*, or perhaps not, as he acknowledges in the 2006 "Afterword." Whether liberal democracy provides this or not, however, is not the essential question. What is more significant is Fukuyama's insistence that the desire for recognition is the most fundamental part of human nature. A major aspect of Voegelin's critique of Kojève's Hegel is that this anthropology is dangerously limited—it takes one goal of human striving and makes it the *only* goal. For Voegelin, human beings desire much more than some abstract "recognition," even if it does have its place in human life. His anthropology is more complete insofar as it is based upon a *hierarchical* understanding of the different human needs and desires. The human being consists of numerous desires and needs, the satisfaction of some being the precondition for the emergence and satisfaction of others. Once the most basic "lower" needs and desires are satisfied, the distinctively human ones can surface. One of these will be the desire for recognition, but this is not all. The human heart has other longings.

For Voegelin, the highest, most important, and most distinctively human of these desires is ultimately the desire for *transcendent* meaning and purpose, which could *never* be fully satisfied by any particular finite political institution or person. This desire demands an answer to the Leibnizian questions: "What is my place within the cosmos? Why is there something rather than nothing? Why is something as it is, and not different?"[17]

In his book *Transcendence and History: The Search for Ultimacy from Ancient Societies to Postmodernity*, Glenn Hughes has explored this problem in depth. Following Voegelin's insights into the human desire for transcendence, he succeeds in demonstrating, through a thorough analysis of myths, poetry, and art from many historical periods and cultures, that there is a basic human relationship to a trans-finite, trans-spatial, and trans-temporal realm of meaning, which cultures express and symbolize in phenotypically different ways. He argues, "Human fulfillment entails the willing embrace and development of our relationship to the eternal and imperishable ground of existence."[18] Anything less than this willingness to participate in the transcendent mystery of the cosmos will be ultimately unsatisfying for human beings.

Kojève and Fukuyama completely overlook this highest of desires constitutive of human nature properly understood. For this reason, they are unable to understand fully what motivates human beings at a core level.[19] In light of this insight, we might venture to say that the provincialism of Islam, the stubbornness of Catholic Christians, or the refusal of anybody else to conform fully to the modern world, is *fundamentally linked to the reassertion of this desire for transcendent purpose*, which has been repressed in Western secular societies. Even though this desire manifests itself immanently in some cases, in the distorted concupiscential drive to convert or kill the entire globe, there can still be discerned in it the reflection of a supposed divine mission. "Recognition" is a thoroughly inadequate conceptual tool for understanding this phenomenon. Only from the perspective of Voegelin's anthropology and philosophy of history can we understand this correctly.

Following Voegelin, Glenn Hughes recognizes some of the potential dangers inherent in the human orientation toward transcendence and, at the same time, can at least partially sympathize with those who would try to stamp out this orientation in human nature. For, throughout history, the temptation to absolutize and doctrinalize particular symbolizations of transcendent truth—resulting in widespread intolerance, mass murder, and self-righteousness—has always run alongside and competed with healthier and more humble forms of the embrace of transcendent meaning. The tendency to construct "metanarratives" and subsequently impose them on other cultures has always been one of the more tragic civilizational impulses. So the rejection of transcendence in contemporary images of reality is at least somewhat understandable.[20] Yet, both Hughes and Voegelin make a case for not throwing the baby out with the bathwater. They try to show that a rejection of metanarratives does not necessarily entail a denial of transcendence. Metanarratives and the experience of transcendence are in no way equivalent. For Voegelin and Hughes, transcendence does not mean stepping outside of history to contemplate and determine its meaning. Instead, the experience of transcendence always takes place *concretely within* the historical process and is thus subject to *perspectival variability*. In becoming aware of our transcendent orientation, one must keep this essential insight in mind.

NOTES

1. Though the popular media and many prominent international relations theorists have predicted China's rise and domination for years, powerful dissonant voices do exist. See, for example, Peter Ziehen, *Disunited Nations* (New York: HarperCollins 2020). Ziehan basically argues that China is due for a significant reckoning. With a subpar geography, extraordinary levels of debt, limited strategic options, a bleak demographic outlook, and a growing cohort of enemies, Ziehan claims that China will likely experience a catastrophic collapse within the next two decades

2. See Samuel Huntington, *The Clash of Civilizations and the Remaking of World Order* (New York: Touchstone, 1996). Also see John Mearsheimer, *The Tragedy of Great Power Politics* (New York: Norton Paper Backs, 2001).

3. Francis Fukuyama, *The End of History*, xiv.

4. Ibid., xiv–xv.

5. For the foundational treatise on Democratic Modernization theory, see Seymour Martin Lipset, *Political Man* (New York: Doubleday, 1960).

6. Fukuyama, *The End of History and the Last Man* (New York: Free Press, 2006) 143–144.

7. Ibid., 144.

8. Slavoj Zizek, *Living in the End Times*, (New York: Verso Books, 2010) 56.

9. Ibid., 38.

10 See "Afterword" to the 2006 edition of *The End of History and the Last Man*, 341–354.

11. See Francis Fukuyama, *Identity: The Demand for Dignity and the Politics of Resentment* (New York: Farrar, Strauss, and Giroux, 2018).

12. See Fukuyama, *The End of History*, 346.

13. There are, in fact, three other major criticisms to which he responds. These are, first, the problem of democracy at an international level; second, the question of the autonomy of politics; and third, the unanticipated consequences of technological development. Though Fukuyama spends just as much time responding to these other three criticisms, I will only treat the one that has to do with Islam, since it is tied directly to my later discussions of Voegelin and Kojève. At least in the "Afterword" where he mentions these criticisms, Fukuyama does not reject his earlier thesis entirely, but qualifies it considerably, and confesses that "the future is really much

more open than its economic, technological, or social preconditions seem to suggest" (354).

14. Ibid., 347–347.

15. Ibid., 348.

16 Zizek has a very thought provoking analysis of how this multicultural recognition of the Other, predominant in Western liberal societies, can never truly achieve its goal of recognition, since the globalized multicultural society automatically turns personal identity into a "life-style choice," and thereby does away with anything like a truly substantial and authentic identity. Multiculturalism is thus, in his view, self-undermining, insofar as it completely misunderstands how people who belong to particular religious or ethnic groups view themselves. For them, the belonging to a substantial tradition has nothing to do with a "life-style" choice. This would be to introduce into their lifestyle something completely alien to it, namely, a Western focus on individual autonomy. When Westerners call upon the Other to become more tolerant and multicultural, they are doing nothing less than demanding "become like us." Zizek calls this "multicultural racism." See Zizek's discussion of the French anti-veal laws in *Living in the End Times*, 43–53.

17. See Barry Cooper's discussion of Voegelin's philosophical anthropology in *Eric Voegelin and the Foundations of Modern Political Science* (Columbia: University of Missouri Press, 1999), 172–173.

18. Glenn Hughes, *Transcendence and History* (Columbia: University of Missouri Press, 2003*)*, 1.

19. As we will see, Kojève attributes this desire to Hegel's "Unhappy Consciousness," which, according to him, has been overcome in Hegel's system. The case of Fukuyama is a little bit different. The only mention of the possible need for a transcendent purpose to human life in the entirety of the *End of History* can be found in a short footnote (n. 7) from page 176, in the context of a discussion of a speech by Abraham Lincoln and the *thymotic* ground of the desire for recognition. This footnote reads, "Lincoln's reference to his belief in a just God, however, raises the question of whether the greatest acts of thymotic self-overcoming need to be supported by belief in God." This passage shows that the question of the transcendent meaning of human life and political order is, at best, a peripheral issue for Fukuyama. Religion is ultimately just about "identity" and "recognition" for him, as it was for Kojève. This, as I will argue, is a fundamental distortion of the meaning and significance of transcendence. In this view, "religion" merely acts as a support for an entirely *immanent* thymos. It has its source entirely in the immanent thymotic subject. Both of these readings have their roots in the typical atheist reading of Hegel's work, which seems to be, unfortunately, the default mode of much Hegel scholarship.

20. Hughes, *Trancendence and History*, 14–15.

Chapter 2

The Origins of a Hegelian Misunderstanding

One thing Voegelin, Francis Fukuyama, and Kojève have in common is that they trace the origins of the End of History concept back to Hegel's philosophy of history. This genealogy is not without justification, as Hegel's *Vorlesungen über die Philosophie der Geschichte* explicitly mentions *das Ende der Geschichte*. In these lectures, Hegel explains that the Napoleonic Empire, which represents the "germ" of the posthistorical political regime, is the final manifestation of *Weltgeist* and must be appropriately understood as such. What he calls the "Germanic Spirit" has succeeded in reconciling all of the contradictions and antagonisms of previous civilizations insofar as it has taken the principle of Protestantism—that man *qua* individual is entirely free in his relationship to the absolute—and given it concrete immanent actualization.[1]

But there are ambiguities and problems in Hegel's presentation of this notion, especially when viewed in light of other aspects of his work.[2] How, for instance, is one to understand Hegel's no less forceful assertions that the Subject is essentially *negativity* or that the course of Spirit is the *continual process* of positing contradictions, overcoming them, and positing new ones? Would this not undermine any belief that history will end in some static, homogenous, and universal regime, where all human strivings and desires are nearly fulfilled? If the human being is essentially negativity—that is, if the human being ceaselessly strives to overcome externality as manifested in the political, cultural, and social institutions of a given regime—then would it not be too far-fetched to believe that the modern world will only give rise to further higher contradictions, ones for which Hegel knew he would not be able to account—say, for instance, the political tensions caused by multicultural and multiracial societies or climate change? Is it possible that Hegel himself, despite—nay, *because of*—his claims to Absolute Knowledge, was

17

aware that the future contained political and cultural possibilities unknown and unknowable to him?[3]

In light of these hermeneutical ambiguities, it is revealing that there is one more thing Voegelin and Fukuyama have in common, which is not quite as apparent on the surface of their work: the *assumption* that Alexandre Kojève's interpretation of Hegel's philosophy is *accurate* and *definitive*, or at least has captured the essence of Hegelian speculation—that is, has brought "Hegel up to date."[4] This assumption results in several more about the meaning of numerous crucial ambiguities in Hegel's texts, rendering them, it is true, very clear, but narrowly and superficially understood. Kojève's analysis of Hegel in his lectures compiled in *Introduction à la lecture de Hegel*, while very insightful, involves a misunderstanding of many vital aspects of Hegel's philosophy. In later chapters, I will identify these aspects and suggest—though not fully explicate, as this would require another full-length study[5]—alternative readings of Hegel which would render Voegelin's criticisms much less effective and reveal a Hegel who is much closer to Voegelin's position than to Kojève's or Fukuyama's.

Before doing this, however, we must take a closer look at the unfolding history of Voegelin's stance on Hegel. The original aim of Voegelin's projected six-volume *Order and History* was to show that the "order of history emerges from the history of order." The first three volumes of this series—namely, *Israel and Revelation* (1956), *The World of the Polis* (1957), and *Plato and Aristotle* (1957)—followed through with this intention. Yet, surprisingly, the fourth volume—*The Ecumenic Age*, published in 1974—showed a radical "break" from the original project. Early reactions sought to explain the meaning of this "break" either in terms of a shift away from traditional or orthodox understandings of Christianity or as an effort to describe in more detail, *from the perspective of consciousness,* the *process* of differentiating consciousness.[6] Certainly, in *The Ecumenic Age* we get a new "theory of consciousness," which is, as John Corrington remarks, "firmly grounded in, and insists upon a return to, original experience."[7] But this book is undoubtedly more. As an effort to distance his work from the abstractions and systems of eighteenth- and nineteenth-century philosophy, this return to "original experience" is meant to ground consciousness, not in some systematic whole that thought must *completely* penetrate, but in the bodily, finite, and concrete life of an individual living within what Plato called "the metaxy." Also, and perhaps more importantly, as a rejection of finality, of systematicity, of the possibility of objectively writing anything even resembling a unilinear historical account, *The Ecumenic Age* is primarily a critique of Hegel and anyone who thinks like him.

Why does Voegelin single out Hegel for especially harsh treatment in this work, especially considering that other thinkers—such as Comte, Marx, and Condorcet, whom he also mentions but does not critique at much length—have, in his view, been guilty of similar errors? Voegelin had criticized Hegel before *The Ecumenic Age*, though not necessarily for the same reasons, and definitely not in such detail and length. One might say that what had changed was the particular tone he adopted and a certain emphasis on him as the archvillain of modernity. Voegelin perhaps singled out Hegel because he represented the high point of what a deformed intellect could become. His depth of understanding was so great, his intellect so powerful, his historical knowledge so detailed, that his insidious influence was much more deceptive. Voegelin chose to single out Hegel because "we do not want to be spared by our best enemies, nor by those whom we love thoroughly," as Nietzsche would have it.[8] Voegelin chose Hegel as his "best enemy" because he loved him and felt a certain kinship within him. While many scholars have sought to understand the significance of this change in Voegelin's thought and its implications for historiography, few, if any, have asked about the specific cause which motivated it. Which specific thinker or book, one should ask, acted as the catalyst for this mature understanding of Hegel? What had happened in the long interval between the publication of *Plato and Aristotle* in 1957 and the publication of *The Ecumenic Age* in 1975?

Professor Thomas Altizer, a close friend of Voegelin and one of the only reviewers to be honored with a response from Voegelin himself, remarked in very blunt terms that the criticisms outlined in *The Ecumenic Age* amount to an "absurd" and "grotesque" misunderstanding of Hegel's thought. He also points out that Voegelin fails to see that he is himself Hegel's direct descendant. As he states, "Voegelin's hatred of Hegel is an attempted Oedipal murder of his Father."[9] In his response to this review, Voegelin commends Professor Altizer's sensitivity to the "central problem" of *The Ecumenic Age*. He thus admits that the question of Hegel's influence on contemporary theoretical derailments was front and center in his mind when he wrote the volume and that the validity and long-term legitimacy of his study stands and falls with this question. First of all, he says, his aim was not to "attack" Hegel, but simply to submit key passages of his work to the same philological and theoretical analysis which he uses on other writers. If the analysis' conclusions are less than sympathetic, Voegelin argues, one might attribute this more to the "difference of spiritual stature" between Hegel and other thinkers than to the difference in their intellectual acumen or power of mind. His ultimately negative view of Hegel does not imply that the latter's texts are worthless or that one cannot learn a great deal from them. On the contrary, Hegel's work is a treasure chest of insights that informed much of Voegelin's own work. Yet, as Voegelin comments, there is a "story" to his relationship with Hegel:

For a long time I studiously avoided any serious criticism of Hegel in my published work, because I simply could not understand him. I knew that something
was wrong, but I did not know what. There was a thinker whom I admired for
the political acumen of his study on the English Reform Bill of 1831, and for
his qualities as a German man of letters which he displayed in his essay-review
of *Hamanns Schriften* (1828), a thinker whom I consulted at every step in my
own work because of his vast historical knowledge and his powerful intellect,
and who at the same time baffled all my efforts at following the thought process
of his dialectics or at understanding the experiential premises of his system.[10]

Voegelin sought to understand Hegel at an "experiential" level—that is to say,
he wanted to discern the preconceptual motivations for Hegel's work. His
unfamiliarity with this precise motivation prevented Voegelin from writing
extensively on Hegel earlier.

But something changed in the years leading up to the publication of *The
Ecumenic Age*. Voegelin must have had an insight that justified his extensive
comments on Hegel after and including the publication of *Hegel: A Study in
Sorcery* in 1971.[11] What was this exactly? The first breakthrough in his understanding came when, after a reading of Baur's *Christliche Gnosis* (1835), he
realized that Hegel's contemporaries viewed him as a gnostic. This insight
helped him to understand a passage from the preface to the *Phenomenology
of Spirit,* which he had previously overlooked—specifically, Hegel's explicit
declaration that he wanted to advance beyond philosophy, the mere love of
wisdom, toward actual knowledge. This insight, however, did not clarify
all that was ambiguous and obscure. There was still much to understand,
including the origins of Hegel's dialectics in Neoplatonism. In addition,
according to Voegelin, the *Encyclopaedie* became much more comprehen-
sible when he placed it in succession to the Neoplatonic encyclopedism of
the Enlightenment Philosophes. The third find which solidified his grasp of
Hegel's thought was the latter's declaration that the *Phänomenologie* was a
work of "magic."[12] All three of these aspects—its relationship to Gnosticism/
Hermeticism, Neoplatonism, and the encyclopedic tradition—combined to
offer a more coherent explanation of the "experiential motivations" underlying Hegel's work.

Nevertheless, there was one more influence who, above all the rest, helped
Voegelin to grasp Hegel's thought in its totality: Alexandre Kojève. In a
very unambiguous and straightforward passage in his response to Professor
Altizer, Voegelin states that this "new awareness" of the true experiential
motivations of Hegel's thought "was stimulated, and materially supported, by
a closer study of Kojève's *Introduction*."[13] This is not the only place where
Voegelin has commented on the immense importance of Kojève's lectures for
his understanding of Hegel. Near the end of "On Hegel: A Study in Sorcery,"

he mentions in a footnote that he views Kojève's *Introduction à la lecture de Hegel* as the indispensable "code" that helps one to crack Hegel's system. "The code is *indispensable* to every serious reader of the *Phänomenologie*; it should be appended to every future edition of this work."[14] Kojève's work was the "break-through" in Voegelin's understanding of Hegel which would later come to present the central issue of *The Ecumenic Age*.

I am not the first to notice the close link between Kojève and Voegelin's understanding of Hegel. Barry Cooper, in his essay "Decrypt: Voegelin and Kojève's Hegel," outlines the very same sequence in Voegelin's gradual discovery of Hegel's experiential motivations, and provides a summary of the general contours of Voegelin's critique of them. As he states, "For most of his intellectual life, Voegelin seemed to be ambivalent about Hegel. It was not until his 1971 essay 'On Hegel: A Study in Sorcery' that he was able to sort out the various dimensions of Hegelian speculation in a satisfactory way. . . . Voegelin acknowledged that his mature understanding of Hegel 'was stimulated and materially supported' by Kojève's Introduction."[15] Cooper notes that as late as 1965 in "What Is Political Theory?" Voegelin referred to Hegel as a "great thinker." While he was often critical of him up to this point, he was generally positive in assessing Hegel's overall accomplishment. This means that the catalytic event that stimulated his later uncompromisingly critical stance toward Hegel occurred sometime between 1965 and 1971, at least eight years after the publication of *Plato and Aristotle* and at least three years before his "break" with the publication of *The Ecumenic Age*. This timeline seems to suggest that not only did Kojève's *Introduction* have a transformative effect on Voegelin's mature view of Hegel, but it also may have at least partially inspired the "break" with the original conception of *Order and History*. For, he phrases the criticisms of his own project in the very same language as his criticisms of Hegel's.

We can corroborate this assertion by juxtaposing the opening paragraphs of *The Ecumenic Age*, in which Voegelin explains the reasons for his break, with some of the major criticisms of Hegel outlined in *On Hegel: A Study in Sorcery*. The original conception of the program, according to Voegelin, assumed the principle that "the order of history emerges from the history of order." *Order and History* was thus an attempt to write a unilinear narrative from which one would be able to discern the general structures of meaning in the primordial "community of being," made up of Man, God, World, and Society. He conceived this narrative as a process of "increasingly differentiated" insight into the order of being in which man participates by his existence. Any order to be found in the process, including but not limited to the digressions and regressions from the heightened differentiation, would emerge if the principal types of man's existence in society, as well as the corresponding symbolisms of order, were presented in their historical succession.[16]

He could not bring this study to its projected conclusion, however, since he realized the structures that emerged from the historical order and their symbolizations proved more complicated than he had expected. These historical materials were "refractory" insofar as they resisted the original six-volume plan he had laid out, which would have narrated from the beginning with the Cosmological empires of the ancient near east and ended with the modern nation-state and the emergence of Gnosticism as the symbolic form of order. This was not to say that the study's principle was wrong, but simply that the sheer number of historical societies and the veritable infinitude of historical facts made it utterly impossible for a human being to penetrate the object of study conceptually. If he had stuck with the project's original outline, it would have been necessary to fit all of this refractory material onto the limited unilinear progression he initially imagined. But this would have amounted to a gross distortion of the material. He would have overlooked certain facts, distorted others, or simply falsified the material involved. As Voegelin comments,

> What ultimately broke the project . . . was the impossibility of aligning the empirical types in any time sequence at all that would permit the structures actually found to emerge from a history conceived as a "course." The program as originally conceived, it is true, was not all wrong. There were indeed the epochal, differentiating events, the "leaps in being," which engendered the consciousness of a Before and After and, *in their respective societies*, motivated the symbolism of a historical "course" that was meaningfully structured by the event of the leap. . . . There was really an advance in time from compact to differentiated experiences of reality and, correspondingly, an advance from compact to differentiated symbolisms of the order of Being. As far as this line of meaning, drawn by differentiating events in the time of history, was concerned, the program had a solid core; and by the same token, the analyses contained in the first three volumes were still valid as far as they went. Still, the conception was untenable because it had not taken proper account of the important lines of meaning in history that did not run along lines of time.[17]

The program's major problem became apparent to Voegelin because of two different, but inextricably linked, reasons: First, due to its immensity, the historical material proved too unmanageable for a single person. Second, to experience the inadequacy of his original project in the face of this vast historical material, Voegelin needed to be conscious of theoreticians' tendency to attempt to compensate for their limitedness by falsifying the historical data. He would later call this tendency "Historiogenesis."

The tendency to try to fit recalcitrant historical material onto a unilinear history conceived as a "course" leading up to the author's present was something he accused Hegel of indulging in to an extreme degree. Three years before his comments on the break with his project, he wrote in regard to Hegel: "The *Phänomenologie* is indeed an 'unintelligible' book, because Hegel cannot go too far in exhibiting his *modus operandi*. In the present instance, he could not simply say: I am going to falsify history in open existence until it fits into my history in closed existence."[18] The entirety of Hegel's corpus, according to Voegelin, is a fundamental distortion of reality, an attempt by an alienated and spiritually defective individual to impose some sort of invented or imagined meaning and order, conceived from the perspective of the "closed existence" of second reality, onto the actual, real, concrete substance of history existing in "first reality." Several experiential motivations underlie the effort to falsify historical facts so that they fit onto an imagined unilinear course culminating in some "end of history" in the author's present. First, there is the need to overcome spiritual alienation through self-salvation. Second, there is the megalomaniacal self-perception as a "reconciler," as a savior of the world, or even as a Christ figure. Finally, there is the inability to bear uncertainty or mystery.

Voegelin's discernment of his own incapacity to master all of the historical materials with which he had to work in a way that would align them with the original conception of his project does not mean that he thought someone else of superior mental capacity could. It was not an act of humility relative to other philosophers with higher cognitive abilities. On the contrary, Voegelin's concession was an act taken *on behalf of mankind as a whole*. It was an admission that no human being, no matter how powerful the intellect, is capable of mastering the infinitude of historical materials in such a way as to put an end to the historical process. Hegel, thus, claims to have done what no man is capable of doing. Voegelin's acute awareness of this fact, as well as the interest in understanding the "experiential motivations" that compel individuals to attempt this impossible feat, induced him not only to resist his own temptation to attempt a similar historical construction, but also to pursue this "central problem" further in *The Ecumenic Age* and the writings that follow it.

The next part of this study will explore Voegelin's concept of "Historiogenesis." It will examine the elements of what Voegelin would consider "healthy" historiogenetic constructions—that is, those that contribute to order on an individual and societal level—as well as those of the defective ones that deform the personality. A crucial element of Voegelin's critique of Kojève's Hegel is the claim that Hegel belongs in the latter group. As we will see, Hegel's writings on history are embedded within a tradition of Christian eschatological reflection, which distinguishes between the sacred and profane layers in the historical process. This tradition is vulnerable to pneumapatholigical distortions for reasons I will outline. Voegelin argues that Hegel appropriates this tradition and, in significant ways, attempts to go beyond it.

NOTES

1. Georg W. F. Hegel, *The Philosophy of History*, tr. J Sibree (New York: Dover Publications, 1956), 103.

2. I am, of course, not the first to notice the problems with Kojève's interpretation of Hegel, nor am I the first to see that Kojève is at least partially responsible for spreading the "end of history" myth as it has to do with Hegel's philosophy. See, for instance, Eric Michael Dale, *Hegel, the End of History, and the Future* (Cambridge: Cambridge University Press, 2014). In his rather thorough treatment of the status of the End of History thesis in Hegel's corpus, Dale points out that it was primarily Kojève, Nietzche, and Friedrich Engels who were responsible for its popular dissemination, though it was exclusively Kojève who inaugurated the French revival of Hegelianism and its subsequent spread to and appropriation in the United States, most notably in Francis Fukuyama's *The End of History and the Last Man*. Even so, Dale concludes that "Kojève's is by far the least convincing account of Hegel's actual arguments about history," as he bases his interpretation of the historical themes in Hegel's philosophy on the identification of Time and the Concept at the end of the *Phenomenology of Spirit* and the presupposition of the centrality of the *Herr-Knecht* struggle (master-slave dialectic). See page 81.

3. See, for instance, Eric Dale's discussion of the future in Hegel in, *Hegel, the End of History, and the Future*, 219–210. Dale insists that because, for Hegel, Philosophy is "its own time comprehended in thought," it is only warranted in making claims about what has happened up to its own time. It cannot go any further. It is impossible to discuss the future prospects of history for the simple reason that the future has not happened yet. Though Hegel does know that Spirit will continue to realize itself in the future, he cannot tell us how it will come about, beyond telling us how it has come about *thus far*.

4. See Barry Cooper, *The End of History* (Buffalo: The University of Toronto Press, 1956), 103.

5. For a more exhaustive treatment of Hegel's End of History thesis, see Reinhart Klemens Maurer, *Hegel und das Ende der Geschichte* (2d ed., Freiburg, Munich: Alber, 1980). For a treatment of how this End of History thesis relates to the work of Alexandre Kojève, see Philip T. Grier, "The End of History and the Return of History," in *The Hegel Myths and Legends*, ed. Jon Stewart (Evanston: Northwestern University Press, 1996), 183–198. Also, see Dale, *Hegel, the End of History, and the Future*, 81–109.

6. For an example of a critical reaction from a Christian, see Bruce Douglass, "Symbols of Order," *Christian Century* 93 (1976): 155–156; also see Thomas J. J. Altizer, "A New History and a New But Ancient God? Voegelin's The Ecumenic Age," in *Eric Voegelin's Thought: A Critical Appraisal*, ed. Ellis Sandoz (Durham:

Duke University Press, 1982), 179–188. For a more recent and more balanced response from a Christian perspective, see James Rhodes, "Christian Faith, Jesus the Christ, and History," in Eric Voegelin's Ecumenic Age: A Symposium, 44–67.

7. See John William Corrington, "Order and Consciousness/Consciousness and History: The New Program of Voegelin," in *Eric Voegelin's Search for Oder in History*, ed. Stephen A. McKnight, 163.

8. Nietzsche, *Thus Spoke Zarathustra*, 46.

9. Altizer, "A New History and A New But Ancient God? Voegelin's The Ecumenic Age," 186.

10. Eric Voegelin, "Response to Professor Altizer," in *Published Essays, 1966–1985*, 296.

11. See Voegelin, "On Hegel: A Study in Sorcery," in *Published Essays, 1966–1985*, 213–255.

12. Voegelin, "Response to Professor Altizer," 296.

13. Ibid., 297.

14. Voegelin, "On Hegel: A Study in Sorcery," footnote 18, on page 251. My emphasis.

15. Barry Cooper, "Decrypt: Voegelin and Kojève's Hegel," 5.

16. Voegelin, *The Ecumenic Age*, 45.

17. Ibid., 46. My emphasis.

18. Voegelin, "On Hegel: A Study in Sorcery," 249.

PART II

Hegel and the Crisis of Christian Salvation History

Chapter 3

Universal History Reimagined

The traditions of religious, cultural, and political institutions put limits on human beings. In this limitation, they reveal their paradoxical tragedy. They restrain and root us—infusing meaning and value—while also prejudicing us and instilling their inherent bias. The identity they impart divides human consciousness, allowing for community and commonality with others on the one hand, while at the same time drawing attention to differences at the source of conflict and violence on the other. From them, we inherit rituals, patterns of behavior, and subconscious attitudes toward others and ourselves. Importantly, they have unique configurations of history that define the terms of our relationships to other societies and cultures, as well as to other individuals living within them. The question of tradition—what they are; how they develop; how they understand themselves in respect to other competing traditions—is thus intimately connected to the question of history itself. It imposes on us several related questions: To what extent is the writing of history possible? How much do the various shades of meaning in a tradition's understanding of the past color its view of the present? These traditions bequeath their values and behaviors to us, down through the ages and, for better or for worse, condition us in ways we may never appreciate, including the manner in which we write history. To fully appreciate the long saga of eschatological identity politics, it is imperative to appreciate the specific traditions out of which it emerged.

Even at the earlier stages of his career, Voegelin, as a product of the Western cultural heritage, found himself concerned primarily with the problem of the traditional Christian understanding of history—comprehended as a unilinear development leading from the creation of human beings, to the fall, the redemptive act of God's self-sacrifice, and up to the existence of the Church as the representative of God's will on earth. As a critical historian and philosopher, he was acutely aware of the myriad distortions to which this history was subject, not only from ideologists concerned with rationalizing a certain political platform or scientific theory but even from within the Christian tradition itself.[1] Indeed, as Voegelin consistently maintained throughout his career, Christianity's vision of history set the stage for the more radical historical distortions of the modern age, including secular eschatological speculation. By distorting the symbolisms St. Paul used to describe the experience and vision of the resurrected Christ—in essence, turning them into doctrine expressed with a foreign pseudo-philosophical vocabulary—the Western Christian tradition created the conditions for its own collapse. It now became just another *doxa* among many.[2] This new doctrinal Christ introduced into the consciousness of Western societies a proclivity toward apocalypticism, millennialism, and eschatological new "Christ" movements. It made possible Hegel's declaration that history had ended in his system.

As early as the 1940s and 1950s, these issues were at the forefront of Voegelin's thought. In *From Enlightenment to Revolution*, a portion of the unfinished and posthumously published *History of Political Ideas*, he reflected at length on the inadequacy of the Augustinian and Neo-Augustinian constructions of history—later adopted as the semiofficial theoretical statement on the Church's historical self-understanding. These histories confronted serious opposition during the early French Enlightenment. Voegelin comments:

> We do not find before 1700 a comprehensive interpretation of man in society and history that would take into account the constituent factors of the new situation, that is: the breakdown of the Church as the universal institution of Christian mankind, the plurality of sovereign states as ultimate political units, the discovery of the New World and the more intimate acquaintance with Asiatic civilizations, the idea of a non-Christian nature of man as the foundation for speculation on law and ethics, the demonism of the parochial, national communities and the idea of the passions as motivating forces of man.[3]

From Voegelin's perspective, the Western Church—before, during, and after the eighteenth century—had failed to keep pace with the historical discoveries of the age, which called for a novel interpretation of sacred history taking these new discoveries into account. Bossuet's *Discours sur l'histoire universelle*, published in 1681, was considered the last attempt at writing a traditional Christian history, consisting of a chronological survey of events from Adam's fall up until the Holy Roman Empire of Charlemagne. In this conception, "the history of Israel, the appearance of Christ, and the history of the Church are the meaningful history of mankind, while profane history with its revolutions of empire has only the function of providing the educative tribulations for Israel and the Church preparatory to the ultimate triumph."[4] The deep-seated issue here, unaddressed by Bossuet, was the growing influx of materials from so-called "profane history." Knowledge of China, India, Russia, and the Americas was becoming more detailed, and this rapid increase in historical knowledge forced upon Western consciousness the realization that the self-styled "sacred history" taking place in the West was in reality only a very minute and inconsiderable portion of the entirety of pragmatic events on the world stage. While Western Europe continued its primarily self-absorbed journey through history, neglecting the importance of countless other civilizations and societies on the other side of the globe, these latter civilizations managed to survive and thrive, and understood their own historical courses as meaningful. This despite the fact that, from the perspective of Europeans thousands of miles away, they were a negligible scrap of "profane" history.

Notwithstanding Voltaire's attempt, in his *Essai sur les moeurs*, to rewrite humanity's history from a non-Christian and hence non-Eurocentric perspective, a new universal history was elusive. His attempt was also awash with prejudices, misunderstandings, and complete disregard for the integrity of past and parallel civilizations and traditions. His fault: he warped history to fit a progressivist schema culminating in the French Enlightenment. His history of the *esprit humain* follows the evolution of opinion as it becomes increasingly refined and provides the general categories within which later secularistic constructions of history would operate. According to his account, from the perspective of the *Siècle des Lumières*, we can observe the meaningful course of history as the "spectacle of errors and prejudices." Over this course, men will "enlighten themselves by their record of misfortunes and stupidities, societies will rectify their ideas, and man will begin to think."[5] Though encompassing a wider historical horizon, Voltaire, just as much as the traditional Christian historians, relegates certain societies, civilizations, and traditions to the abyss of irrelevance, or at best to the position of a necessary stepping-stone to his own present generation. Not only does Voltaire fail to overcome the problems that beset traditional Christian historiography, he also falls victim to many of the same ideological constructions. As Voegelin observes,

> The meaning of history on this intramundane level is constructed as an analogue to the Christian meaning so closely that we can trace the parallelism step by step. In any construction of a meaningful universal history, in the first place the object that shows a meaningful structure has to be constituted as a whole. In the Christian system, the whole is constituted through the idea of creation and the descent of mankind from Adam; in the secularistic construction, the whole is evoked as a totality of empirical knowledge. The ideal of empirical completeness which appeared as a degenerative substitute for Christian universality, of no more than transitory importance, becomes the secularistic analogue of the divine creation of mankind if it is coupled with a new construction of historical meaning.[6]

Voltaire constitutes the "whole" of his historical meaning by, first, declaring *empirical completeness* to be the sole criteria by which historiography should be judged and, second, arbitrarily deciding that the historical progression toward the emergence of historians like himself is the meaning of universal history. This enlightened empirical thoroughness will supposedly result in more refined, tolerant individuals and societies. Here we see that Voltaire, like the Christians whom he opposes, displays a tendency of many ideological historians: *he selects a partial structure of meaning, declares it to be total, and arranges the rest of the historical materials around this preferred center of meaning.*[7]

Although written at an early stage in his career, Voegelin's reflections on Bossuet and Voltaire prefigure many of the more conceptually refined insights into history and consciousness later found in the five volumes of *Order and History*. In the introduction to the *World of the Polis*, he revisits this problem in the context of his own attempt to write a history of order. To avoid the pitfalls of both Voltaire and the Neo-Augustinian Bossuet, a historian must somehow account for the validity and integrity of traditions and histories running parallel to each other in time. He must affirm the reality of the "leaps in being," as the events in particular cultures that gain a higher differentiation of the truth of reality and constitute a true "before" and "after" in the particular tradition from which they emerge. The difficulty is accomplishing this feat without simultaneously assigning to any one of the traditions an ultimate status. At the same time, he must avoid the equally damaging temptation to allow each of these traditions a radically equal status. Despite the limitations of the traditional Augustinian history of mankind, one must, according to Voegelin, acknowledge that it at least struggled with the *real issue* of spiritual substance. In this respect, the Voltairian history, though richer in historical detail, was fundamentally inadequate. As Voegelin remarks, "But the blow was no sooner delivered than it was clear that even a defective construction, which had at least a grip on the problem, was better than the dilettantic smartness of phenomenal argument."[8] The Augustinian conception of the course of history was more successful than the Voltairian since it dealt with the myriad theoretical and spiritual problems that arise with the tension between world-immanent and world-transcendent purpose. Even if it did not ultimately succeed, it at least refrained from eclipsing the transcendent purpose of history in its analysis and did not declare itself to be the final and definitive statement on the issue, but was structurally open to higher theoretical advancements.

The problem Voegelin faced is a serious one: how can one write a history of mankind—including traditions stemming from Western, Near-Eastern, Far-Eastern, and Russian societies, as well as perhaps societies and traditions yet unknown because hitherto undiscovered—in light of the Augustinian conception of the *Historia Sacra*? This is to ask whether one can retain the symbolism of a Christian sacred history without indulging in the temptation to elevate the pragmatic Christian European-centered tradition to the status of ultimate truth. This history would have to accomplish several things: First, it would somehow allow for the emergence of new structures of meaning, that is, for future "leaps in being," without giving in to the temptation to completely relativize the previous ones. Second, it would deal adequately with the problems and tensions of a historical process that is neither completely immanent nor transcendent. Finally, it would do justice to particular, concretely living human beings, neither seeing them as "stepping-stones" to some end of history in the present age, nor assigning to any one individual a savior status.

According to Voegelin in the *World of the Polis*, one of the greatest attempts at rewriting the *historia sacra* came in the nineteenth century in Hegel's corpus. Hegel definitively expanded representative history beyond the Judeo-Christian sacred history by demonstrating the participation of *all human societies* in the unfolding of *Logos* in time. In this sense, he actually succeeded, at least more than the traditional Augustinian configuration of history, in endowing every concrete human being with some essential dignity and purpose, as everyone participated in the *Logos* to some degree. The relative success of this enormous enterprise was simply incredible, according to Voegelin, as far as the inclusion and diagnosis of phenomena were concerned. As he comments, "In spite of such handicaps, the Hegelian genius for discerning the characteristics of each level of intellectual and spiritual order has achieved feats of insight to which even contemporary historians and philosophers might have recourse with profit more often than they do."[9] In 1956, when Voegelin published the *World of the Polis*, he seems to accord Hegel exuberant praise.

However, the cause of Hegel's ultimate failure, according to this account, was his attempt to reduce the *Logos* of revelation to the *Logos* of philosophy, and the *Logos* of philosophy to the dialectics of consciousness. Philosophy (*Liebe zum Wissen*) was supposed to advance toward Gnosis (*wirkliches Wissen*). This feat could only be accomplished by "anaesthetizing" the philosopher's sensitiveness for the borderline between the knowable and the unknowable. While elsewhere Voegelin would also suggest that human beings participate in the divine *Logos* through Reason, he was not willing to go quite as far as Hegel in using the language of "identity-in-difference" to talk about the relationship between the divine and human *Logos*. Terminologically, "Participation" must be carefully distinguished from "identity-in-difference." For Voegelin, only the former constitutes the fundamental human experience, since the term indicates there is an element of the unknowable in reality without at the same time barring all of reality from intellectual penetration.

Although it is true that human beings, by means of the concept of Being, are oriented toward the totality of all that is, including divine reality, this orientation alone does not necessitate the possibility of complete conceptual comprehension. What Hegel does is transform the incarnation of Christ from the *mystery* of God's presence in history into the appearance of the identity-in-difference of God and man. This transformation acts as one of the unjustified premises of Hegel's system. As Voegelin remarks,

> The superbly skillful manipulation of the gnostic symbolism could, of course, not abolish the mystery—either of the order of being, or of an historical mankind—but the sheer massiveness of the dialectical work, the vast expansion of the gnostic opus to the limits of the phenomenal world, could push the mystery so far out of sight that the impossible at least appeared to have become possible: the philosopher's Logos in possession of Being.[10]

While the substance of this critique is structurally similar to the one Voegelin will voice in "On Hegel: A Study in Sorcery" and *The Ecumenic Age*, there are some definite differences, which are likely the result of both his lack of a fully conceived philosophy of consciousness and his earlier admission that he had not yet fully understood Hegel. Hegel's work, at this point in Voegelin's understanding of him, is still marked by extreme "ambiguity." In this less developed view of Hegel, Voegelin attempts to make sense of his system as a modern manifestation of acosmic, ahistorical cosmological myth: "Gnosis is a speculative movement within the form of the myth; and modern Gnosis, as the Hegelian identifications show, is a throwback from differentiation into the pre-historic compactness of the myth."[11] Yet, this designation would prove inadequate. Voegelin would never again try to understand Hegel's system in this way. The constructions that went into Hegel's new *historia sacra* would prove to be much more complex, and his *psyche* more deformed. Indeed, the full scope and implications of the issues Hegel raises, as well as a very tentative solution to them, are not presented until 1974 in *The Ecumenic Age*. More specifically, Voegelin's development of the concept of Historiogenesis and his distinction between two fundamental types of history are central in his enterprise to understand Hegel as a human being and the *historia sacra* he attempted to construct. Voegelin insists it is impossible to understand fully the modern Gnostic "philosophies of history"—as exemplified in Kojève's Hegel—without having an adequate conception of their Christian predecessor. The modern "philosophers of history," who have attempted the feat of writing a new *historia sacra,* have failed for many of the same reasons Christianity itself had failed. They overlooked the unique relationship between the individual historian—who as an embodied human being necessarily belongs to a particular tradition within a particular society—and "mankind" as a whole, which can never be reduced to a datum of experience on which speculation is possible. The complexities of this relationship give rise to two types of historical symbolism: there is, first, the history *internal* to a tradition and, second, the history *into which this tradition comes and out of which it passes*. I will call the first type of history "tradition-bound history" and the second genuinely "universal history," which Voegelin will characterize as "a mystery in the process of revelation." A detailed unpacking of the notion of Historiogenesis will clarify this distinction further.

NOTES

1. The only full-length treatment of Voegelin's take on the development of the Christian tradition is Jeffrey Herndon's *Eric Voegelin and the Problem of Christian Political Order*. This book details Voegelin's analysis of the origins, development, and climax of the medieval Church in his *History of Political Ideas*, with particular emphasis given to the problematic relationship between the "apoliticism" of the Christian ideal and the unavoidable requirements of living in the political world. While this book is valuable as a study of Voegelin's earlier thought, it does not in any way take into account some of Voegelin's reconsiderations of his intellectual enterprise. To be specific, Herndon fails to mention that from the perspective of Voegelin's later thought, the history of Christendom found within the *History of Political Ideas* is an historical construction, plagued by the misguided attempt at arranging the events of "Christianity" and "Western civilization" on a unilinear timeline from a beginning to an end, with the aid of imagination and convenient oversight.

2. Eric Voegelin, *The Ecumenic Age* (Columbia: University of Missouri Press, 2000), 91–94.

3. Eric Voegelin, *From Enlightenment to Revolution*, (Durham: Duke University Press, 1975) 5.

4. Ibid. 6. Voegelin quotes Bossuet in a footnote: "Ainsi tous les grands empires que nous avons vu sur la terre ont concourru par divers moyens au bien de la religion et à la gloire de Dieu, comme Dieu meme l'a déclaré par ses prophètes" (Bossuet, *Textes Choisis et Commentes par H. Bremond* [Paris, 1913], 2, p. 58). It is interesting that if one substitutes "Hegel" for "Dieu" in this passage, there are striking similarities to passages from Kojève's *Introduction*. Cf. Barry Cooper, *The End of History: An Essay on Modern Hegelianism* (Toronto: University of Toronto Press, 1984), 224.

5. Ibid., 10.

6. Ibid., 10.

7. Ibid., 11.

8. Eric Voegelin, *World of the Polis* (Columbia: University of Columbia Press, 2000), 82.

9. Ibid., 83.

10. Ibid., 84.

11. Ibid., 85.

Chapter 4

Elements of Historiogenesis

As we hinted earlier, historiogenesis is the ubiquitous tendency of political institutions, religious institutions, philosophers, and historians generally to construct an imaginary history that fits discrete events running parallel to each other into a unilinear course leading up to the author's present. By "present" could be understood either the author himself, his particular generation, or a political/religious institution to which he pledges allegiance. Historiogenesis is, to break down the word itself, a "genesis"—that is, a creative act, a making, or a fabrication—of a "history" that is felt to be in some way meaningful. It is the act of tradition-bound historians wanting to endow their particular tradition with the meaning they feel present within it. In this light, tradition-bound history is always to a certain degree imaginative, since the author or institution in question, though not literally producing the "facts" of the past, arranges them imaginatively into a meaningful sequence, something that is only possible by disregarding some "facts" and distorting others.

Many motivations underlie these constructions. As Voegelin outlines in detail, they can result from the natural feeling of anxiety a person feels about the precariousness of his existence and the meaning found within it. In this case, historiogenesis becomes a psychological defense mechanism to deal with the harshness of reality, of the tension of existence out of nonexistence.[1] Alternatively, it can arise from the need to give a more secure foundation to imperial rule. Here, historiogenesis is an attempt to justify the actions of a ruler or government by giving them historical legitimacy.[2]

These motivations need not be understood in a negative light. As it stands, human beings cannot really avoid historiogenesis, simply because they tend to understand their own lives, or the histories of their societies, in a narrative fashion. Narratives, to be successful, must emphasize certain details while obscuring others. They must, to a certain extent, remain blind to the reality that there are countless other narratives being told simultaneously. They must also forget about the tremendous multicausal complexity of the events that constitute the narrative to squeeze them all somehow into a meaningful unilinear course. When an individual understands his own life, he understands it as a story. Some moments will be emphasized as "life-changing," others will be forgotten completely. Societies and religious traditions do likewise.

Even more importantly, other aspects of historiogenesis make it a necessary *precondition* for meaningful personal or social existence. All its manifestations, for example, consist of speculation on the origins and causes of some felt presence of social order or disorder. This sensed presence of order or its lack in society extends into the psyche of the historiogenetic speculator. The historiogenetic construction thus becomes an effort to overcome disorder, a form of disorder itself, or an attempt to *preserve* an experience of order. Additionally, historiogenesis is invariably a speculation on what Voegelin calls the "community of Being," consisting of Men, Gods, World, and Society, elements which make up the structural constants in all hitherto known mytho-speculative narratives. Corresponding to each of the partners in the community of Being, we generally see various cultures engaging in anthropogonic (search for origins of Men), theogonic (Gods), and cosmogonic (world) speculations. Historiogenesis tends to absorb each of these aspects of the search for meaning in history—that is, it uses them in the construction of a meaningful unilinear narrative leading from the origins of the Gods, the Cosmos, and Men, up to the present of the speculator's society. They all nevertheless hold an integrity of their own as quests to understand a meaningful *aspect* of reality. The structural constants underlying the pluralistic manner in which these forms of historiogenesis are expressed exhaust the possibilities of speculation on the origin of Being.[3] These constants, it should be stressed, always exist in the mode of a *questioning search*, to which the pluralistic symbolic expressions serve as answers. We get nowhere, according to Voegelin, by putting the pluralistic symbolic expressions side by side against each other, or by treating them as "opinions" that we can use logic and evidence to confirm or reject. These "answers" to the various modes of speculation on the ground of reality only make sense *in relation to the questions they answer*. The questions, in their turn, make sense only in relation to the concrete experiences of reality from which they have arisen. And, finally, the concrete experiences, together with their linguistic expression, only make sense in the cultural/traditional context that sets limits to both their direction and range.[4] To be sure, this does not amount to a pure relativism. The complex of *experience-question-answer* is itself a constant of consciousness we can find universally across different cultures and traditions.

Because my analysis to this point has remained rather abstract, it might be appropriate to provide some concrete examples to illustrate the various types of historiogenesis Voegelin outlines. As the quintessential example of Theogonic speculation, one could of course point to Hesiod's *Theogony*. Not only is this work a form of mytho-speculation on the origins of the Gods, but it also explores the origins of the cosmos, the emergence of mortal human beings after the long genealogy of Gods, and the societal victory of Jovian *Dike* over the primordial Titanic forces of disorder. We see, therefore, that the *Theogony* is also an Anthropogony and Cosmogony. As another example, we could look at the book of Genesis in the Judeo-Christian scriptures, which contains two complementary myths about the origins of the universe. The first is a macrocosmic perspective on God's performative speech acts that bring the universe, and what order there is in it, into being. It begins with the creation of the Cosmos and climaxes in the creation of human beings: "So God created humankind in his image, in the image of God he created them; male and female he created them."[5] There is a movement, within the same narrative account, from a Cosmogony to an Anthropogony. From a microcosmic perspective, the second myth looks at the origins of human life and the first human disobedience to God. This myth initiates history in the Judeo-Christian sense, to the extent that it constitutes the basic structure of a constant struggle to achieve the original order God ordained for creation. The microcosmic account of creation is therefore a form of historiogenesis—as the search for the origins of order and disorder in society and man—which absorbs into itself an anthropogony and cosmogony.

There are also examples in Eastern cultures. Voegelin analyzes the work of Ssu-ma Chien and his historiogenetic account of Chinese history in the *Shih-Chi.* This narrative reveals the succession of dynasties, unfolding the course of Chinese history from its mythical beginnings down to the writer's own time. According to Voegelin, Ssu-ma Chien arranges the dynasties on a well-structured line to account for the attainment or loss of each dynasty's possession of *Tê*—meaning virtue or power. As Voegelin notes, "The *tê* is the sacral substance of order that can be accumulated in a family through the merits of distinguished ancestors. When the charge has reached a certain intensity, the family is fit to exert the functions of a ruler over society. The *tê* of a ruling family will be exhausted in the end."[6] Though warping historical details, this narrative allowed Ssu-ma Chien to render the meaningful course of Chinese history intelligible. It helped make sense of the rise and fall of the various dynasties that made up this course.

Even more illustrative of the historiogenetic construction is the case of the *Sumerian King List.* For most of its history, Mesopotamia consisted of a plurality of city-dynasties existing simultaneously. Occasionally, one of these dynasties would become powerful enough to subjugate all or many of the others. With this new power arose the need for its historical justification. Voegelin illustrates the case:

Whereas a critical historian would have to relate the parallel histories of the cities, as well as the changes of ascendency, the authors of the King List constructed a uni-linear history of Sumer by placing parallel city-dynasties in succession on a single temporal line of rulers, issuing into the restored empire of their own time. The parallel histories of the cities were abolished, but nevertheless were absorbed into an imaginary, uni-linear history of empire. One cosmos, it appears, can have only one imperial order, and the sin of coexistence must be atoned for by posthumous integration into the one history whose goal has been demonstrated through the success of the conqueror. If it, then, be remembered that the imaginary line of Kings is extrapolated to its absolute point of origin in divine cosmic events, so that nothing extraneous to it has a chance of disturbing the one and only course admissible, the construction appears as an act of violence committed against historical reality.[7]

For these historiogenetic accounts, the symbolizations arise from the *experience of history* and some felt presence of meaning within it. That is, for each account the perception of a meaningful and precarious present, whether at an individual or institutional level, results in an effort to understand or justify the present *status-quo* by placing events and facts on a line of irreversible time.

In every case, to construct a unilinear history is to abstract from the very concrete experiences of the individuals living within a concrete society. These countless individuals have had very complex and multifaceted experiences of the world. Most of them have not left any trace of their experiences beyond their biological life span through a written record. As a result, death consigns them to oblivion. A historiogenetic speculator must voluntarily blind himself to these countless parallel experiences so as to rearrange societal events onto a narrative conceived as a line. *They must forget about the irreducible plurality of lines running through history.* A critical historian could expose these constructions' "factual inaccuracy" by merely pointing out a parallel societal history that it has overlooked. Such was the case with the discovery of the histories of China and the Americas in the seventeenth and eighteenth centuries. He could go even further by highlighting the irreducible plurality of conscious individuals *within* these societies, all of whom presumably conceived of their own lives in a unilinear fashion.

NOTES

1. Eric Voegelin, *The Ecumenic Age* (Columbia: University of Missouri Press, 2000), 123.
2. Ibid., 144–145.
3. Ibid., 111. Voegelin provides a very helpful diagram which lays out the various aspects in the structure of historiogenesis:

Table 4.1

S(t) (t-a,c,h)
S(a) (a-t,c,h)
S(c) (c-t,a,h)
S(h) (h-t,a,c)

In the diagram, "S(x)" denotes the speculation on the aspect of the community of being in question. "t," "a," "c," and "h" stand for Theos (the Gods), Anthropos, Cosmos, and History respectively. It is important to keep in mind that although a single author may privilege one aspect of the community of being over the others in his speculations, all are generally included. So, for example, despite the fact that S(t) privileges a search for the origin of the Gods—as for instance in Hesiod's *Theogony*—it will also include speculations on the origin of humans (a), the cosmos (c), and society (h).

4. Ibid., 125.

5. Genesis 1:27.

6. Voegelin, *Ecumenic Age*, 346.

7. Ibid., 115.

Chapter 5

Tradition-Bound Historiogenesis

Christian Historia Sacra

To further clarify tradition-bound historiogenesis, let us now look at the work of two recent historians—namely, Regus Brubaker and Eric Rebillard—who draw attention to the historiographic tendencies outlined above in their studies of early Christianity. Using the term "groupism," Brubaker has indicated the inclination of historians to reify groups and societies. He defines groupism as follows: it is "the tendency to take discrete, sharply differentiated, internally homogeneous and externally bounded groups as the basic constituents of social life, chief protagonists of social conflicts, and fundamental units of social analysis."[1] Attempting to avoid the pitfalls of groupism, Eric Rebillard experiments with what we might call a *bottom-up* approach to historical analysis, applying it specifically to the traditional Christian historical self-understanding. He believes his new methodology is vital in the study of early Christian history because all extant historical evidence, mostly texts composed by clerics, *fabricates* Christian identity along the lines of groupism.[2] With this tendency in mind, Rebillard takes as the underlying presupposition of his analysis the "internal plurality" of the individual—meaning the irreducibility of any individual in religious or political environments to any single unequivocal identity. This presupposition is indispensable to an adequate understanding of the early Church's history, which "groupism" has greatly distorted. As we saw earlier in our analysis of the *Historia Sacra*, traditional Christian historiography would lead one to believe that the early Church was characterized by seamless transition in the apostolic succession, and that this era was the golden age when most converts identified so strongly with their faith they were willing to face martyrdom. Rebillard paints a strikingly different picture. As he comments, "Not only did Christians share a number of identities with non-Christians, but Christians and non-Christians alike did not necessarily or consistently regard their religious allegiance as more significant than other identities."[3] One of the major factors determining the skewed Christian history of the period of persecutions, passed down through the Catholic tradition, was the historiographic work of Eusebius in his *Historia Ecclesiastica*. Eusebius, according to Rebillard, was influenced by contemporary circumstances and unwarranted assumptions about the particular populations he was analyzing. In light of more recent textual evidence, we now know his understanding of Christian history was dreadfully wide of the mark. While Eusebius would have one believe Christian identity was solid and unshakable in the face of Roman persecutions, such was simply not the case. A complex historical reality underlay his simplified analysis of the various persecutions, revealing his many groupist tendencies. As an example, Rebillard notes that in spite of their leaders' incitement to do so, Christians *seldom* opposed a communal response to the persecutors, and a significant number of them temporarily suspended their Christian allegiance. Furthermore, when Decius issued the order that every inhabitant of the Roman Empire must sacrifice to the gods for restoration of order, the *vast majority* of Christians complied, since they considered the sacrifice a requirement of their membership in the imperial commonwealth.[4] We get a portrait of an extremely complex and diverse early Church, consisting of members who identified with more than one part of the ethnically, politically, and religiously multifaceted landscape. Groupist and historiogenetic tendencies obscure this great complexity.

The ideal image of a Christian Roman Empire, treated as a single religious community, was no more than a historiogenetic construction, the product of Eusebius's pen at the urgings of Constantine. In words reminiscent of the *Sumerian King List*, Eusebius describes how under one God reigned one emperor, who called himself "bishop of those outside the church."[5] As another recent historian, Garth Fowden, would describe the issue,

> Before Constantine, Christian congregations enforced their decisions by excluding those who did not comply. Under Constantine, the church succumbed to the temptation to repress its deviants, and with fatal logic made the emperor God's active representative on earth. With this move, the theoretical preconditions for the conversion of Rome into a single homogeneous religious community had been met.[6]

This situation makes clear to us the radical separation between the words, declarations, and symbolic actions of the Church or Christian emperors and the actual course of historical events as they took place on a pragmatic level. By the sixth and seventh centuries, lists of councils, with their canons, had become a standard way of claiming authority in doctrinal matters. But conflicts emerged where two equally authoritative figures in the Church claimed to have tradition on their side. For example, John Scholasticus and Eutychius, rival patriarchs of Constantinople in the late sixth century, drew up *competing* lists of conciliar decisions to support their *opposing* positions. As an instance of a similar problem, once the Church had begun trying to define the nature of God in formulas that had to be generally agreed upon, the inevitable result was intense competition in which every participant and every group resorted separately to the authority of tradition.[7]

The point of these historical examples is to demonstrate that Voegelin's concept of historiogenesis provides us with a useful methodological tool for analyzing the reasons these historians have a tendency to overlook the vast complexity of the events they preserve. What, for instance, could motivate someone to deliberately construct a unilinear history extending from the creation of Adam to an imagined Roman institutional *status quo*, when it is not altogether obvious that this line is the only one that exists? How, furthermore, was it possible for various figures within these competing strands of Christianity to appeal to the authority of tradition and apostolic succession, when they were more or less aware that their competitors in other sects were engaging in the very same thing?

As I mentioned earlier, it would perhaps be a misreading of these historiogenetic constructions to see in them some sort of self-serving and malicious intent. Much to the contrary, we discern in them an attempt at understanding or justifying a present that is experienced as meaningful. But this meaning is expressed in symbolically different ways. As Averil Cameron remarks, "This is no romanticizing of the past, but rather its practical adaptation to the needs of the present. . . . [T]hey wished devoutly to connect with a past they still saw as part of their own experience and their own world. . . . [A]s they saw it, it had not so much to be remade as to be reasserted."[8] The past and the present were felt to dissolve into one another in meaningful present experience. The goal of looking to the past was not "accuracy"—understood in the sense of aligning propositions about facts with their reality—but rather to deal with the richness and significance of the present.

This unique type of Christian historiogenesis is not exclusive to the early Church communities. This construction has remained in Western consciousness to the present day, most notably in the theology and self-understanding of Roman Catholicism. This despite the increasingly detailed knowledge of Western history in the twentieth century. Yves Congar, an influential twentieth-century Dominican theologian, gives a very lucid and differentiated account of the meaning of tradition and its corresponding history as the Roman Catholic Church understands it. For him, tradition is the *continual* presence of a spirit or moral attitude across generational and national divides. It is both unwritten—to the extent that individuals embody it in words, deeds, and rituals—and it is written—insofar as it can sometimes only be successfully transmitted across generations through the documents of the Magisterium, liturgy, or catechisms. For Congar, "[t]radition is an offering by which the Father's gift is communicated to a great number of people throughout the world, and down the successive generations, so that a multitude of people, physically separated from it by space and time, are incorporated in the *same, unique, identical* reality."[9] Several historiographical presuppositions skew Congar's view of Christian history. He believes in the continuity of the Church and its efforts to pass on the "deposit of faith," which was given to it directly from Christ and the apostolic succession. Congar constructs a unilinear history by aligning all of the elements of his understanding of tradition onto a line conceived as a course. In the context of a discussion about this "deposit of faith," Congar describes how "we may speak of a unique subject of tradition, including its source even, coming right down to us, like a wave unfurling from its point of origin to the shore. The source is the prophets and the apostles as witnesses of Jesus Christ."[10] The symbolic image used here, of a wave continuing on its course from an epicenter to its destination, is a perfect case in point of the necessity of imaginative obscurity in any historiogenetic account of history. These types of images must be used in order to conceal the rich reality underlying it. The image distorts, simplifies, and eclipses the historical course it purports to describe. There can be no "history," understood in terms of a course, without the myriad distortions the metaphorical aspect of language provides. This twentieth-century attempt to reduce the Church to the same self-identical monolithic entity is yet another example of historiogenesis. As the work of Rebillard, Averil Cameron, and Garth Fowden shows, the Catholic—not to mention Christian—tradition has always been far from achieving the status of universality, comprised as it is of members with very complex and multifaceted identities, thoughts, and beliefs.

It is important for our analysis to remember that all of the traditional mytho-speculations and histories we have been inventorying help provide the traditions in question with structural matrices of meaning within which the actual writing of "history"—as the arrangement of events or facts on a line— can occur. These "histories" play a large role in endowing political events, religious ceremonies, or simple day-to-day activities with a high degree of significance. They *ground* the various traditions that come to influence the unique manner in which a historian thinks about and structures his historical narrative, while at the same time *emerging* from this same narrative. There is a relationship of *mutual* influence and structural *codeterminacy* between these traditions and their unique historiographies. A Catholic Christian understanding of history, for instance, is determined by certain traditional presuppositions; and these presuppositions have largely emerged from its historiography. As finite and concrete human beings living in finite and concrete societies, historians cannot extricate themselves from the cultural inheritance and modes of thought or belief with which they were born.

Following Voegelin, the conclusion we can draw from the preceding examples is that it is impossible for a historian to gain some supratraditional standpoint from which to assess other traditions side by side with his/her own. Though one might opine on the meaning of the "history" of Mankind as a whole, including traditions and peoples one has never encountered, this attempt will always be tinged by the historiographic presuppositions of one's particular tradition. This is precisely what has happened in all of the historiographic constructions we have just examined. From a limited traditional standpoint, each historian pronounced on the meaning of the history of mankind, but in so doing merely created a unilinear history of his/her respective tradition. To use the terminology formulated earlier, these historians try to transform their tradition-bound history into the genuinely universal history of mankind. From within a limited historical perspective, each has imagined himself, at least implicitly, into the position of God overlooking the course of history as a whole. Though one might believe a modern critical historian to be an exception to this rule, considering he tries to do justice to the "facts" without any distorting influence from his subjective "values," the issue is much more involved. For this attempt at doing justice to the facts is always undermined by the sheer infinitude of facts to which a historian has very limited access. He thus cannot overcome this partial and restricted position in a tradition of historiography. Voegelin suggests, therefore, that all history is in some way a form of historiogenesis.

NOTES

1. Cited in Eric Rebillard, *Christians and Their Many Identities in Late Antiquity: North Africa, 200–450CE* (Ithaca: Cornell University Press, 2012), 2.

2. Ibid.

3. Ibid., 7.

4. Ibid., 7.

5. Eusebius, *The Life of Constantine*, 4.24. Cited in Garth Fowden, "Varieties of Religious Community," in *Interpreting Late Antiquity: Essays on the Postclassical World*, ed. G. W. Bowersock, Peter Brown, and Oleg Grabar (Cambridge: Belknap Press of Harvard University Press, 2001), 89.

6. Fowden, "Varieties of Religious Community," 90.

7. Averil Cameron, "Remaking the Past," in *Interpreting Late Antiquity*, 5.

8. Ibid., 1–2.

9. Yves Congar, *The Meaning of Tradition* tr. A. N. Woodrow (San Francisco: Ignatius Press, 2004), 12. My emphasis.

10. Ibid., 49.

Chapter 6

Gnostic Historiogenesis

The Case of Hegel

The seeming inevitability of historiogenesis raises many questions. Are there differences among its various forms? Is there some standard by which we might assess the relative acceptability or impropriety of its cases? In particular, is it possible to say that certain brands of historiogenesis—say, the Catholic Christian—are more truthful or less of a construction than others—for example, the Enlightenment Progressivist? In more blunt terms, are some forms more dangerous than others? In these questions lies the key to fully appreciating the complexity and nature of Voegelin's critique of Hegel and the notion of the end of History.

One could criticize Voegelin's hyperbolic lashing of Hegel by highlighting the resemblance of the latter's historical construction to other equally distorting constructions, which Voegelin apparently finds much more acceptable. Why, one could ask, is Voegelin so harsh with Hegel's historiogenetic construction when Christianity and Mesopotamia engaged in precisely the same thing? To answer this question, let us first lay out some of the details and peculiarities found within Hegel's historiogenetic construction. After explaining these details, we can then contrast Hegel's construction directly with the Christian one to figure out precisely why Voegelin condemns the former more harshly than the latter.

Because the eighteenth century had broken with the traditional Christian construction of history—as exemplified in the work of Bossuet—a new tradition-bound historiography was needed that could take all of the new empirical advances into account. The parallel histories of China and India, the Islamic world and Russia, had emerged in so obvious a way that a philosopher of history could no longer ignore them. However, Voltaire's new historical construction ultimately failed, despite its more complete empirical knowledge. It was not until Hegel's arrival in the nineteenth century that we would get a serious attempt at a historiogenetic account that dealt with the

spiritual substance of mankind. Hegel wanted to continue the Christian historiogenetic symbolism on the new level of a Neoplatonic, immanentist speculation on the *Geist* (Spirit) that dialectically unfolds in history until it reaches
its full self-reflective consciousness in the wake of the French Revolution
and the Napoleonic Empire. From this imperial present, Hegel dealt with a
manifold of pragmatic events even less amenable to a unilinear course than
the parallel histories of the Sumerian city-states. Like the Sumerian court
priests, Hegel also had to distort the historical material and overlook certain
unwelcome facts. But now these facts spanned an entire globe rather than a
small region of the Near East. He achieved this feat by interpreting the great
civilizational societies as successive phases of the unfolding of *Geist* (Spirit).[1]

Voegelin underlines Hegel's treatment of Mesopotamia and Egypt as
examples of the historical distortion needed to create his new form of historiogenesis. If one were to do justice to the facts, these civilizations would
have to be placed at the beginning of Hegel's timeline. But this, in Hegel's
narrative, would have disturbed the westward march of empire toward
ever-increasing freedom. He imagined the process proceeding from China
and India, through Persia, Greece, and Rome, to the Germanic world with its
climax in the empire of the French revolution. As Voegelin comments,

> Hegel resolves the problem by demoting the early near-eastern empires to
> subsections of the later Persian empire that had conquered them; and the same
> fate he inflicts on Israel and Judah. By ingenious devices of this kind—the
> inclusion of "Mohammedanism" in the "Germanic World" deserves to be
> remembered—he manages to herd the errant materials on the straight line that
> leads to the imperial present of mankind and himself as its philosopher. The
> modern technique of historiogenetic construction, it appears, is still the same
> as the Sumerian.[2]

Hegel's new *historia sacra* follows the same general contours as every
form of historiogenesis, failing to do complete justice to the "facts." This
narrative inevitably ends in the author's present age, when history has supposedly ended.

Kojève's influence on Voegelin's view of this historiogenetic construction is enormous. Kojève's commentary is limited to the *Phenomenology
of Spirit*, but it begins and ends in much the same way as the historiogenetic construction outlined in *Die Vorlesungen über die Philosophie der
Geschichte*. By means of his own form of mytho-speculation, he gives the
historical construction more adequate theoretical backing. It begins with a
mythical anthropogony—which, as a reader of Kojève later finds out, is indistinguishable from a theogony—in which the first human beings, emerging
from Consciousness to Self-Consciousness, fight to the death in the pursuit

of "la reconnaissance" (recognition). For Kojève, this "désir anthropogène" (anthropogonic desire)—that which constitutes human nature properly understood—marks the transition point to history properly understood—"*l'histoire human est l'histoire des Désirs désirés* (human history is the history of desired desires)."[3] Human beings will not be satisfied, and thus will continue to strive for a better and more rational world, unless political institutions arise that can accord universal recognition to every single human being. Whereas the biblical understanding of history's motor-force sees human beings in a perpetual struggle to regain the order God had originally established for them in some prehistoric paradise, Kojève's Hegel sees its propulsion in this desire for recognition. To construct this history and prove that it had ended in his System, Kojève's Hegel had to misconstrue the errant historical "facts" to arrange them on a line leading up to his present historical situation, the Napoleonic Empire. He could only do this in light of a philosophical anthropology based solely upon the myth of his anthropogony. He can only prove that human nature is completely satisfied at the end of history if he has already explicated and "justified" what would satisfy it.

The culmination of history in the Napoleonic Empire is according to Kojève, the subject of section C, chapter 6 in Hegel's *Phenomenology of Spirit*. *Geist*, the spirit that has the certitude and assurance of itself, is in the final analysis Hegel himself. Hegel's philosophic system (*Phenomenology* and *Encyclopedia*) is no longer a search for "*la Sagesse*" (wisdom) but "*la Sagesse*" itself. Yet this truth is not universally and necessarily valid until all that was possible has effectively happened.[4] According to Kojève, Hegel's *historia sacra* inevitably and ineluctably leads to this point, when all possibilities for the future have been realized, when, to quote the author of Ecclesiastes, there is "nothing new under the sun." In this logic, novel historical realities are impossible if human nature is completely satisfied. While events may occur and things may happen, nothing wholly new would emerge. This completely satisfying, total, and definitive reality is coextensive with the Napoleonic Empire, the principle of which is now being spread in liberal democracy. To quote Kojève at length, the Napoleonic Empire is

a Universal and Homogeneous State: it unites the entirety of humanity (or, at least, *that part of it which counts historically*) and "cancels" in itself all specific differences: nations, social classes, families. Christianity is itself also "cancelled". There is no longer a dualism between the Church and the State. Therefore, wars and revolutions are henceforth impossible. That is to say that this State will no longer have to modify itself, it will stay eternally identical with itself. Yet, Man is formed by the State where he lives and acts. Therefore, Man will no longer change either. And Nature (without negativity), is in all ways "accomplished" forever. By consequence, the science that correctly and completely describes the Napoleonic World will always remain entirely valid. It will be Absolute Knowledge, the final term of all philosophic research. This Knowledge—it is Spirit certain of itself.[5]

The citizens of this "Universal and Homogeneous State" are completely satisfied at the end of History. One is, according to Kojève, fully and definitively satisfied when one's unique and exclusive personality is recognized by *everyone* in its dignity, value, and reality. The only precondition for this universal recognition is that one also be willing to recognize everyone else. In the Kojèvian anthropology, to be fully satisfied is to be unique in the world but also universally valid. Thanks to the "universality" of the State, one is recognized by, and equal to, everybody else. Because the State is "homogeneous," it is one's true self that is recognized, and not one's family, social class, or nation. The irony here is that at the same time the State recognizes one's particularities one is also losing these particularities as substantial differences (class, culture, family ties, etc.) disappear. The particular "Moi" (me) relates directly to the Universal without screens formed by specific differences. What is more, only in this postrevolutionary world does Individuality emerge for the first time. Kojève concludes that Hegel's lasting accomplishment is to have fully understood this individual, this "homme intégral," this fully actualized human being.

The inconsistent logic of Kojève's commentary is conspicuous. The supposed end of history Hegel outlines is only accomplished when the *Désir anthropogène* is fully satisfied. But who has defined and set limits to this *Désir anthropogène*? Was it not Hegel, or Kojève, himself? Does this philosophical anthropology not amount to an unjustified *presupposition* for Hegel's system, which is supported *solely* through the mythical battle for recognition?[6] The battle, as Kojève's Hegel describes it, never truly happened as an historical event. It is merely the attempt at articulating the essence of a historical epoch (most likely the Homeric age), which, for Kojève's Hegel, is symbolic of mankind's primordial desire. *The fact that Kojève's Hegel takes this epoch to be paradigmatic for all of Mankind reveals an unjustified presumption.* Crucially, it grounds his tradition-bound historiogenetic account of history and allows him to pronounce that history has come to its end. But it does not take a critical historian to notice the dangerous nature of Kojève's claim that there is still a considerable portion of mankind that, in light of this philosophical anthropology, does "not count historically."

Now we arrive at the key question: does this misconstruction of history and human nature warrant Voegelin's uncompromising condemnation, especially since Kojève's Hegel is definitely not the first one to do it? Does not the Christian tradition itself do something similar—namely, espouse an undefended philosophic anthropology grounded in a myth and then declare the end of History to be the "accomplishment" or resolution of all of the tensions and desires expressed in this same anthropology? What precisely is the difference between the two historiogenetic constructions? Thomas Altizer raises a similar problem in his review of Voegelin's *Ecumenic Age*. He acknowledges that the fundamental difference between the two thinkers was Voegelin's rejection and Hegel's acceptance of a unilinear historical construction, but does not proceed to analyze in any depth the similarities and differences between Hegel and other historiogenetic speculators. What is most fascinating is that Altizer proceeds to argue that Voegelin himself displays many more similarities to Hegel than he wishes to admit. As he describes,

> Certainly the Voegelin who believes that what happens in history is the very same differentiating consciousness that constitutes history is a clear descendant of Hegel. Voegelin can even directly follow Hegel in identifying the problem of an "absolute epoch" as the central issue in a philosophy of history; for Voegelin, too, an absolute epoch is understood as the events in which reality becomes luminous to itself as a process of transfiguration. Hegel's philosophy of history is grounded in his identification of the absolute epoch as being marked by the epiphany of Christ. Voegelin refuses to identify the absolute epoch with the epiphany of Christ as a particular event or historical process, identifying it rather with a universal humanity as embodied in the great spiritual outbursts and the universal empires of the Ecumenic Age.[7]

Here Altizer strikes to the core of the main conflict between Voegelin and Hegel: the fact that Hegel's historiogenesis is intimately linked with the Christian one. Then why doesn't Voegelin just condemn Christianity itself? This link is vital. Hegel's placing of the absolute epoch of history in the period of Christ's incarnation—which revealed to mankind the identity-in-difference of God and man—is, as we have seen, nothing else than an attempt to write a new *historia sacra* in light of an increased and more differentiated knowledge of world history. Hegel, despite reacting against the overly mystical and pietistic Christian environment of his time, placed himself squarely in the tradition of Christian historiography. Like his Christian predecessors, Hegel wants to write a history of salvation and God's self-revelation to mankind. However, the similarities end here.

For Kojève's Hegel, the content, *not* the complete form, of truth was fully revealed in the incarnation of Christ. Christianity, the Revealed Religion (*Die offenbare Religion*), holds a central importance not just for Western consciousness, but for mankind as a whole, as it revealed Absolute truth in the form of *Vorstellungen*, Representations or "Picture-thoughts." The *incarnate* divine—as opposed to a separate divine "beyond"—is the fundamental truth and *preliminary* goal of world history. With his wider grasp of historical, literary, and cultural details, Hegel sees this vital truth prefigured in several non-Western civilizations. The "avatars" of the Hindu religions, and most importantly the insight that the "self is Absolute Being" (*das Selbst ist das Absolute Wesen*) attained in the Greek cult forms, herald the coming age of Christ's incarnation. As Hegel states,

> All the conditions for its production are at hand, and this totality of its conditions constitutes its coming to be, its Notion, or the production of it in principle. . . . These forms, and on the other side, the world of the person and of law, the destructive ferocity of the freed elements of the content, as also the person as thought in Stoicism, and the unstable restlessness of the Skeptical Consciousness, constitute the audience or periphery of shapes which stands impatiently expectant around the birthplace of Spirit as it becomes self-consciousness (i.e. around the manger at Bethlehem).[8]

Although Hegel shares with traditional Christian historiography the assumption that world history hinges on the birth of Christ, he differs from it to the extent that he tries to incorporate the freshly discovered civilizations and traditions into his new *historia sacra*. Voegelin admires him for this effort. However, he also sees this Absolute Epoch as a stepping-stone to his own present day, something for which Voegelin condemns him. To be sure, Hegel indeed recognizes the integrity and worth of traditions running parallel in time. This fact cannot be overlooked in any assessment of Hegel's system. Yet despite this inherent dignity, what are in Hegel's mind past, one-sided, or incomplete forms of consciousness are still relegated to an inferior position in history. These forms become the necessary organically interconnected members of the Whole that is Hegel's truth. And though the content of this truth revealed itself progressively through history, and most fully in the incarnation of Christ, it would not take on *final* form until Hegel made the Whole explicit in his system: "This first revelation is itself immediate; but the immediacy is equally pure mediation or thought, and it must therefore exhibit this in its own sphere as such."[9] This shape of Spirit does not yet have the form of the Notion—of systematic conceptual language—something which can only be accomplished in Hegel's system.

In this Hegelian conception, world history then seems to contain not one but *two goals*. In ancient civilizations, the content of *Geist* (Spirit) relentlessly tried to burst forth into human consciousness. It was present in every civilization and on every continent, but was looking for the suitable cultural matrix through which it could reveal itself completely. *Geist* was searching for self-consciousness. We might call this revolution the first goal of history.

Nevertheless, once truth's content became known, the remainder of history turned out to be a search to give this content full and complete expression in the proper conceptual medium. This intellectual feat is only feasible after sufficient time has passed, allowing *Geist* to run through the remainder of its shapes at the level of the new revolution in consciousness. This is the history of Christianity and, subsequently, philosophy. Hegel's philosophic system places itself at the end of this line. It can be seen as the attempt to put together all moments of *Geist*'s self-manifestation in reality. Spirit's full rational content—that is, Reason (*Vernunft*) itself—could only reveal itself gradually because humans, as self-conscious beings, needed time to step back from the immediate experiences to reflect on and give them conceptual precision. Hegel's system is the full self-reflection of Spirit at the end of its historical course.

Notwithstanding the abstract and totalizing nature of Hegel's discourse, Voegelin is mistaken in conceiving Reason (*Vernunft*) and *Geist* as parts of some monolithic institution or tyrannical historical force "marching" through history up to Hegel's present, trampling on insignificant individuals and killing everything in its path. Instead, Reason and *Geist* must be understood concretely, as realities in which every single human being participates. To be human is to participate in them. They cannot be rejected in favor of some irrational or willed faith, since even such rejection would require an explanation of the rationale for doing so.[10] A more honest appraisal of Hegel's *historia sacra* reveals the series of individuals and institutions that participate in, but *ultimately fail* to fully embody, the rational existence for which they were born. Further, political history is the gradual unfolding of rational political institutions until the appearance of the universal and homogeneous state. And the history of philosophy/religion is the *progressively refined* articulation of this truth. As Jean-Luc Gouin would describe it, the mutual refutation of philosophic systems "over the entire course of the history of knowledge bears witness not to the collapse of reason but rather to its excess in increasingly refined apprehensions and in increasingly vast fields."[11] So, although Hegel conceives of history as this progressive unfolding of truth and reason, one is not entitled to say that, in his mind, certain individuals somehow do not matter or are not fully human. Every concrete human being over the course of history participated in reason to some degree, and therefore had some essential dignity. Unlike the traditional Neo-Augustinian reading of history, or even Congar's views on tradition, which harshly condemns to damnation any member of "profane history" who did not have the luck to be baptized into the Catholic Church, Hegel's construction endows every civilization and person with inherent dignity, regardless of time period and position on the globe.

Let us pause briefly to summarize the commonalities in Voegelin's and Hegel's conceptions of history. Both believe humans participate in Reason, though Voegelin is fonder of the Greek term *Nous*. Both attach dignity to the concrete human consciousness over against "groupist" hypostatizations. Both see the activity of the Spirit—or, for Voegelin, the *pneuma*—in all human life. For Voegelin, Hegel's case becomes more complicated when it confronts the issue of the *degrees* of rationality in human life and the question of whether or not a finite human being can actually achieve *full* self-consciousness. One might acknowledge, as Voegelin does, that one cannot authentically give up reason in favor of some vague intuitionism, while at the same time acknowledging one's *failure* to embody fully this rationality or truth one seeks.

In his most essential historiogenetic symbol—namely, the term "Magisterium"—Congar grants to the Church the infallible authority by which its existence might be justified. The Magisterium's role is to transform the "material" tradition—understood as the oral and written deposit of faith given through Christ's revelation to mankind—into "formal" tradition or rules of faith. In his way of thinking, something like the Christological controversies and the councils of the early Church were nothing but opportunities to take what was implicit in the "deposit of faith"—that is, the words and deeds of Jesus Christ—and give them reflective conceptual articulation with the language and theological symbolisms that were available at the time. The Magisterium is what enables the Church to interpret and formulate these rules and dogma accurately. From it derives not only the authority of tradition but also its capacity to be renewed and reinterpreted. It is interesting that this conception is not unlike Hegel's statement that the "content" of truth must be given proper conceptual form.

We can view the historiogenetic symbol "Magisterium" as an attempt to bestow on the institutional Church the authority and historical justification it needs to demand obedience in doctrinal, moral, and cultural matters. On this specific point, there is not much difference between the Church, Sumerian kings, and Hegel himself. But there is one essential difference. The Church, though having this authoritative status, is *not* the final arbiter and full embodiment of truth. Summarizing Aquinas, Congar states,

> With regard to our faith and the position it holds in the present economy, he knows and states that its object or formal motive is uncreated truth, insofar as it is revealed in holy Scriptures and in the teaching of the Church, which flows from this same uncreated truth. But St. Thomas adds that here the Church is only a *secondary rule*, measured by the primary rule, which is divine Revelation. *She is a sort of echo or reflection.*[12]

What distinguishes the Church from many other institutions is the fact that it does not regard itself as the full embodiment of truth and the ultimate goal of history. Instead, it sees itself as the indicator or navigational beacon of this truth, which can only be found *beyond* itself. The historical justification of the Church, therefore, is its role in doing just this, in *pointing beyond itself* to a higher truth and fulfillment. Although this self-justification requires a historiogenetic construction, the meaningful present that motivates the construction is *not in any way construed as the ultimate meaning.* It signifies a higher fulfillment that is to come *in the future.*

Like Hegel's, the Church's historiogenetic construction has two basic goals in history. For both, the first was reached in the self-revelation of God to humanity through the incarnation of Christ. In the Church's understanding, the second goal culminates in the *eschaton,* a time when God's final transfiguration of reality will occur and Christ will return to judge the living and the dead. However, this is crucial: as far as the Church is concerned, this final goal *has not yet come.* The Church's present role is thus to preserve the deposit of the first goal while it *awaits* the second. Compare this second goal with Hegel's own construction, in which the entirety of truth, revealed over the course of history, becomes conceptually articulate in his system. In contrast to the Church, Hegel sees himself and/or his philosophic system as *the ultimate goal of history*—that is, as the event to which everything in the historical process leads. *Hegel does not point beyond himself but rather everything in history points to him.*

Kojève interprets Hegel's system in this specific way: "As for the genesis of Hegel's philosophy, one could say that the entirety of the *Phenomenology* is nothing other than a description of this genesis, which culminates in the production of this same *Phenomenology*, which describes this genesis of philosophy and thus renders it possible by understanding its possibility."[13] Whatever the virtues of Hegel's system, this form of historiogenesis is entirely unacceptable in Voegelin's eyes. To distinguish this Gnostic form of historiogenesis—also seen in the work of Auguste Comte and Karl Marx—from others, Voegelin coins the term "egophany," a word suggesting self-assertion and self-revelation as opposed to "theophany," or divine revelation. While the Church understands its historical role as the preservation of Christ's "theophany," and constructs a historical narrative justifying this role, Hegel believes himself and his system to be the *higher truth* of this "theophany." Hegel's history includes but goes beyond the traditional Christian *historica sacra*, insofar as the latter has *come to an end* in his system. His system does not participate in truth or represent truth—as does the Church's Magisterium—but *is* truth in its complete form. The imaginative historical construction by which the Church articulated its experience of meaning in reality is an assertion about the truth of this reality, which comprises mankind as a whole, but it was not a *self-assertive* construction. Herein lies the fundamental difference between Christian and Hegelian historiogenesis. As Voegelin remarks, thinkers, institutions, and humans generally cannot help constructing imaginative stories of their pasts. Yet "when a thinker, whatever his motives may be, forgets his role as a *partner* in being, and with this role

the metaleptic character of his quest, he can deform the remembered asser-
tive power of imagination in his quest imaginatively into the *sole power* of
truth."[14] In Voegelin's understanding, Hegel is not just guilty of asserting a
truth about the historical course of mankind. He does something much worse.
He imaginatively transforms this assertion into a *self-assertive* absolute truth.
In other words, he invents a *second* imaginative construction on top of his
first. Hegel, thus, is guilty of eclipsing the fundamental *participatory* reality
of human existence.

NOTES

1. Eric Voegelin, *The Ecumenic Age* (Columbia: University of Missouri Press,
2000), 116.
2. Ibid., 116.
3. Alexandre Kojève, *Introduction à la lecture de Hegel*, ed. Raymond Queneau
(Mesnil-sur-l'Estrée: Gallimard. 2001), 13.
4. Ibid., 145.
5. Ibid., 145. My translation from the French.
6. As Eric Michael Dale comments, the primary defect of Kojève's interpretation
is that he reads the entirety of Hegel's system through the lens of the Herr-Knecht
(Master-Slave) dialectic. "Once the pernicious struggle between the master and
the servant is overcome, history has achieved its zenith and the concept's process of becoming has come to an end" (Dale, *Hegel, the End of History, and the
Future* [Cambridge: Cambridge University Press, 2014], 81).
7. Thomas J. Altizer, "A New History and a New But Ancient God? Voegelin's The
Ecumenic Age" in *Eric Voegelin's Thought: A Critical Appraisal*, ed. Ellis Sandoz
(Durham: Duke University Press, 1982) 186.
8. Georg W. F. Hegel, *The Phenomenology of Spirit*, tr. A. V. Miller (New York:
Oxford University Press, 1977) 456.
9. Ibid., 461.
10. Jean-Luc Gouin, "Der Instinkt der Vernuftigkeit: De L'Inaliénabilité de la
Rationalité," in *Hegel-Studien*, Band 44, January 29, 2010; 4.
11. Ibid., 3. My Translation from the French: "Et les refutations de celles-ci tout
au long de l'histoire du savoir témoignent non pas de la faillite de la raison, mais
bien plutôt de son dépassement en des appréhensions toujours plus affinées et en des
champs toujours plus vastes."
12. Yves Congar, *The Meaning of Tradition* tr. A. N. Woodrow (San Francisco:
Ignatius Press, 2004), 69–70. My emphasis.
13. Kojève, *Introduction à la lecture de Hegel*, 161. My translation from the
French: "Quant à la genèse de la philosophie de Hegel, on peut dire que tout la PhG
n'est rien d'autre qu'une description de cette genèse, qui culmine dans la production

de cette même PhG, laquelle décrit cette genèse de la philosophie et la rend ainsi possible en comprenant sa possibilité."

14. Eric Voegelin, *In Search of Order* (Columbia: University of Missouri Press. [author: please supply date]), 55.

Chapter 7

Historical Mankind and Historical Traditions

With the insights from the preceding chapters in mind, let me venture a few tentative conclusions. Catholic historiogenesis, like most others, does not conceive of itself as merely a narrow traditional understanding of historical events, limited to a particular context in time and space. Rather, it views the *historia sacra* as a history of Mankind as a whole, in which *all* human beings, civilizations, and societies participate. From its present situation, felt as meaningful and worth preserving, it retrospectively extrapolates events to their divine-cosmic origins. The aura of meaning radiates from this point of origin to all humankind. In this sense, Catholic historiogenesis does not differ in any way from other traditional historiographies. As one living within a tradition that had come to be defined by this unique historiography, Voegelin attempted to come to terms with the unavoidable finitude that would restrict the scope of his historical vision. In so doing, he formulated a symbolism that would retain the peculiar essence of his own tradition while at the same time doing justice to the integrity and *mystery* of the history of Mankind. The inescapable tensions between traditional histories and the history of mankind, which can never be fully known, gave rise to a new symbolism in his thought that simultaneously preserved, challenged, and transcended traditional Christian categories.[1] According to Voegelin, the history of mankind is a mystery in the process of revelation, and as long as one lives in time, within a particular tradition, one cannot know its ultimate origins and goal. The best and most responsible way to approach the question of history is to acknowledge the incompleteness of any historical account without giving up the effort to write it entirely. It is an unavoidable aspect of the human condition, arising from the experience of meaning and its process of development, which cannot simply be thrown out as nonsensical and futile. Yet at the same time, one must approach writing history with "fear and trembling," knowing

61

that the narrow perspective of our traditions may lead us into error just as easily as to salvation.[2]

For Voegelin, we are participants in a field of history we cannot master completely. We can lay out the rules one must follow in order to participate effectively in the game, but this game has no scoreboard indicating to us the remaining time or probable victor. It extends into an unknown future in which other participants will surely emerge and pass away. It stretches into an unknown past from which we ourselves have emerged to play our very limited role in the game. But the game itself encompasses every one of its participants. Thus, the acceptability of a historiogenetic construction depends on the degree to which it acknowledges itself to be a participant in the common endeavor of mankind to understand the history of mankind. Voegelin's major issue with the secularized eschatological philosophies of history becomes clearer, then, as the allegation that they aim to abolish completely the tension between traditional-bound historiography and the universal history of mankind through a self-assertive act of self-salvation. In these deformed historiogenetic constructions, end of history speculators fail to see themselves as participants. Instead, they imaginatively put themselves in the position of one who could oversee the game and determine its final result.

NOTES

1. I am fully aware of the proximity of this language to the meaning of Hegel's *aufheben*.
2. Psalm 55:5; Philippians 2:12.

PART III

Intentionality and the Historical Process

Chapter 8

Voegelin on Human Consciousness

When we distinguished in the last chapter between egophanic histories and other more self-transcending ones, we hit on a core element in Voegelin's critique of Hegel. But the root of this distinction is buried still deeper. Submerged beneath the superficial veneer of philosophical "opinions" and "assertions" about meaning lies a concrete human being and his psychological disposition. Specifically, in the last section, we did not investigate the structures in human consciousness that affect its ability to understand history in the proper way.[1] In this next part, we will plunge deeper into this issue. I will argue that end of history speculators radically distort the historical process by reducing it to a phenomenological object in the external world about which speculation in the mode of intentionality would be possible. I will illuminate the consequences of this distortion.

Without doubt, Voegelin's theory of consciousness is the central starting point for his more mature reflections on history, politics, and society. As early as the *New Science of Politics* in 1951, Voegelin recognized that a theory of politics, if it was going to penetrate to principles, also had to be a theory of history.[2] In the later *Anamnesis*, he reorders the priorities. Here, both a theory of history and a theory of politics must be first and foremost grounded in a philosophy of consciousness.[3] This task occupied him until his death in 1985 and found its fullest expression in the incomplete and posthumously published *In Search of Order*, the fifth and final volume of *Order and History*.

Voegelin's philosophy of consciousness is the result of a lifelong struggle with the implications of Husserl's theory of intentionality.[4] In his ongoing dialogue with Alfred Schutz, we come to see a man who recognized there was something fundamentally limited in Husserlian intentionality analysis but who was at a loss as to how to articulate an alternative successfully. This task was especially difficult since it was the very attempt to use linguistic symbols to describe consciousness and history—which are not datums of intentional experience—that seemed to change what he was struggling to describe into an "object" or "thing" in the mode of intentional experience. This inadvertent transformation validated his hesitations about phenomenology as the standard philosophical approach. Human experience is not exclusively a consciousness of immanent objects in the world. Yet, there is something innate to consciousness predisposing it to distort its experiences in this way. How are we to grasp conceptually this predisposition? Voegelin's later thought explores the possibility of using language to express alternative modes of consciousness that do not fall into the trap of "thingifying" all of reality. As we will see, it is possible that language—and, most importantly, the abstractions it makes possible—is primarily responsible for changing dimensions of consciousness and experience which are not and cannot be objects of focal awareness. The danger, he will allege, is that language may condition us to mistakenly believe *all* realities are possible objects of intentional consciousness.

Crucially, Voegelin recognized that the intentional mode of consciousness was the fundamental mode of Hegelian speculation. And so, its limitations allowed Hegel, and other egophanic historians, to distort the dialectics of Time. This distortion, along with the other key ingredient of messianism, led to Hegel's egophanic historiography. In the most general terms, the fundamental issue with Hegel's philosophy of history—deriving from his failure to understand consciousness properly—is that he treats the dialectics of Time or History as if it were an object or "thing" of the external world, having its own discernible *telos*. This error depends upon viewing the substance of history in the mode of intentionality.

In the Foreword to *Anamnesis*, Voegelin describes the ongoing development of his views on consciousness. Even as early as the 1920s—during his brief sojourn in the United States, where he was able to research and write *Über die Form des Amerikanischen Geistes* (1928)—he became aware of the irredeemably "poor state" of political science and the need to ground it in a new philosophy of consciousness. Neo-Kantian theories of knowledge, value-relating methods, historicism, descriptive institutionalism, and ideological speculations on history had gone so far in "disfiguring" the realm of science that only a colossal effort to both dismantle these inadequate theories and develop a viable alternative could actually succeed in reestablishing it on a stable footing. The results of his first attempt to articulate a philosophy of consciousness were still valid, he alleged. The difficulty was that, at the time of this effort, he lacked the historical and philosophical knowledge that would have enabled him to move beyond mere criticism toward his own developed theory. The most important result of these efforts was

> the insight that a "theory" of consciousness, in the sense of generically valid propositions concerning a pre-given structure, was impossible. For

consciousness is not a "given" to be deduced from outside but an experience of participation in the ground of being whose logos has been brought to clarity through the meditative exegesis of itself. The illusion of a "theory" had to give way to the reality of the meditative process; and this process had to go through its phases of increasing experience and insight.[5]

These early insights crystallized in the volume *Anamnesis*, a collection of meditative experiments aiming to unearth these experiences.

Voegelin's philosophical dialogue with Alfred Schutz began in their student days at the University of Vienna and continued until Schutz's death in 1959. All three of the texts contained within the first part of *Anamnesis*, entitled "Remembrance," date from this early period, between 1938 and 1959. However, the core insights developed in these texts originate from a particular conversation they had in New York City in 1943, which clarified for both of them the questions they were pursuing in methodologically different ways. Schutz came at them from the perspective of phenomenology and Voegelin from the perspective of classical philosophy. Voegelin's key insight was this: phenomenological philosophizing such as Husserl's is in principle oriented toward the model of the experience of objects in the external world, while classical philosophizing about political order is in principle oriented toward the model of noetic experience of transcendent divine being.[6] The words of a recent phenomenologist clarify the orientation of phenomenology: "All our awareness is directed towards objects. . . . Every act of consciousness, every experience, is correlated with an object. Every intending has its intended object."[7] For Voegelin, on the contrary, it is simply not the case that all our experiences are experiences of objects. Schutz had a similar insight. He recognized that the great obstacle to the development of a thorough phenomenology was the problem of the transcendental ego and intersubjectivity, on which Husserl in his *Méditations Cartésiennes* had already stumbled. Schutz realized that the egological derivation of intersubjectivity had to be abandoned and that it was necessary to posit the social world as a *historical given* that is impenetrable to phenomenology.[8] Both Schutz and Voegelin were thus approaching the limits of phenomenological speculation.

The two texts of most concern to us are Voegelin's correspondence letter on Husserl's *Krisis der Europäischen Wissenchaften* and his essay "On the Theory of Consciousness." Both display Voegelin's early attempts at articulating a theory of consciousness in response to the previously recognized limitations of Phenomenology. In the correspondence letter, Voegelin explicitly praises Husserl's subtle analysis of the problems with the Galilean scientific paradigm that later led to physicalism. He also admires his treatment of transcendental subjectivity as the theme of philosophy since Descartes and his elaboration of the "transcendental ego" as the founding of the objectivity of

the world. In all of these respects, Voegelin is "more than willing to recognize
this essay as the most significant achievement in epistemological critique of
our time."[9] Nevertheless, this essay's major shortcoming had more to do with
its "image of history." Husserl, like so many others, claimed that his phenomenological methodology marked the culminating point in the history of philosophy. But it was apparent to Voegelin that Phenomenology did not exhaust
the entire range of philosophic endeavor. Epistemological critique is neither
an independent topic nor a sphere in which all other philosophical problems
are rooted. If it had been, laying the foundation of an epistemological critique
would also mean laying the foundation of philosophy.[10] Epistemological
critique must be rooted in a broader ontology that results in a more adequate
philosophy of history.

Husserl's distorted image of history sees the relevant history of mankind
consisting of Greek antiquity and the modern age since the Renaissance. As
Voegelin mockingly describes this Husserlian history, Hellenism, Christianity,
the Middle Ages—an insignificant timespan of no more than two thousand
years—are a "superfluous interlude." Likewise, the Hindus and Chinese are,
for Husserl, no more than a curiosity on the periphery of the globe. In the
center of the world stands Western man as man per se. Following Hegel's
Modus Operandi, Husserl himself picks and chooses whatever historical data
suits his purpose. For him, because man is a rational creature, "philosophy
and science are the historical movement of the revelation of universal reason."[11] With the Greeks, the *telos* of mankind achieved its breakthrough. In
Voegelin's own words,

> After the initial foundation of philosophy by the Greeks and the interval of
> two thousand years, during which this entelechy evidently amused itself else-
> where, its modern reestablishment has been implemented by Descartes. This
> modern Cartesian reestablishment went awry due to certain imperfections,
> masterfully analyzed by Husserl. Kant made a good partial beginning to bring
> philosophy back on the right track. We skip the philosophy of German Idealism
> and Romanticism; this brings us to philosophy's final foundation, embodied in
> Husserlian transcendentalism.[12]

The sarcasm in this description is unmistakable: Husserl, like many of his
philosophic predecessors, places himself squarely at the end of a philosophic
history, claiming to have brought it to its conclusion and thereby to have
inaugurated a new era. It is yet another case of historiogenesis, of selecting a
partial account of the meaning of historical development and making it total.

In his capacity as a historiogenetic speculator, Husserl sees himself as a
"functionary of mankind." This self-designation reminds one rather force-
fully of the more murderous functionaries of the twentieth century.[13] Voegelin

attributes this poor use of historical and philosophical terminology, not to any malevolence on Husserl's part, but simply to naïveté and the very narrow philosophical concerns with which Husserl dealt. Husserl seemed blithely unaware that the meaning of human history cannot be exhausted by the history of an epistemological problem. Because Husserl's collectivist *telos* is ultimately rational in nature, the problem of philosophy is identified with the problem of spirit in general. And insofar as spirit is the substance of man, it is identified with the problem of man in his fully developed form.[14] Husserl himself summarizes this reduction in one of the most quoted passages from the *Crisis*: "The true spiritual battles of European humanity as such are fought as the battles of philosophy."[15] Mankind as a whole, which can never be an object of speculation, is here reduced to European mankind, and must be distinguished, according to Husserl, from "merely anthropological types." To quote from the *Crisis* at length,

> Only then [when Husserl brings the teleological development of modern philosophy to its conclusion through his apodictic epistemological foundation] could it be decided whether European humanity bears within itself an absolute idea rather than being a merely anthropological type like "China" or "India"; it could be decided whether the spectacle of the Europeanization of all other civilizations bears witness to the rule of an absolute meaning, one which is proper to the sense, rather than the non-sense, of the world.[16]

Not only does Husserl overlook the bloody pragmatic details involved in the "Europeanization of all other civilizations," but the concept of "mankind" appears to be reduced to a community of individuals engaged in philosophizing with one another. The philosophical *telos* of history is shifted once again to an intramundane collectivity, much like the collectivities of the Marxist proletariat, the German *Volk*, and Mussolini's *Italiana*. This reduction necessitates the *historical irrelevance* of the vast majority of human beings and human societies, who become "merely anthropological."[17]

It is necessary to link Husserl with other messianic speculations about the end of history that have emerged in the nineteenth and twentieth centuries. As Voegelin states,

> Husserl's apodictic history is, just like Communism's "genuine" history, not a continuation of empirical history (note Husserl's passionate refusal to allow his teleological interpretation of history to be countered with empirically historical arguments). Instead of being a continuation, it is a transposition of history to a new level of revelation of the human spirit, with which begins a new apodicticity. Husserl's radicalism has, aside from the specifically problematic component of transcendental subjectivity, a messianic component on the strength of which

the final foundation becomes, with its apodicticity in the historically social realm, the establishment of a philosophic sect at the end of time.[18]

Though perhaps more benign in his intentions, Husserl commits the same theoretical error as Hegel, Auguste Comte, Marx, and Lenin. The egophanic assertion that characterizes all of these thinkers, the pseudo-messianic quality in their work, undermines their true theoretical achievements, or at least forces one to look at them with a skeptical eye.

However, apart from his asserting it, Voegelin has not yet shown that intentionality—understood on the model of a transcendental subject contemplating immanent phenomena in the world—is limited in the philosophical problems it can treat. Voegelin must illuminate the *other fuller dimensions* of consciousness. He begins to work this problem out in "On the Theory of Consciousness," the theoretical prologue to the following anamnetic experiments. Here, Voegelin demonstrates with theoretical rigor that the transcendental subject is *not* the apodictic starting point of human consciousness. He suggests, in fact, that consciousness—as well as the traditions and cosmic whole in which it participates—are *givens* in experience. The subject thus does not "constitute" them. *These realities of consciousness are received. Human consciousness is fundamentally receptive at its core.*

Voegelin calls this aspect of human consciousness its "luminous" dimension. Consciousness is not just an active intending of objects, whatever they may be. It *passively* receives various experiences or insights completely independent of its intentional mode of consciousness. Robert McMahon explains,

> Intentionality proves more familiar experientially than luminosity because we necessarily pay attention to whatever we intentionally do. Nevertheless, luminosity is no less fundamental to consciousness, even though we advert to it less often. It seems to feature the receptivity of consciousness in apprehending the real, rather than its activity. Its general model-experiences would include poetic inspiration, intellectual insight, and aesthetic arrest.[19]

In poetic inspiration, for instance, the poet seeks to simply *allow* the words and verses to flow through him, as if an external agent (e.g., the classical muse) uses the poet as a mere means. As Bernard Lonergan's work shows, one could apply the same observation to the achievement of intellectual insight. The philosopher, scientist, or layman may have all of the evidence in front of his face. That is, he may consciously intend all of the information he needs in order to have the insight. Yet the insight might not come. The person in question might not experience that act of supervening understanding which sees the pattern or meaning of the data in front of him. When he does finally have the insight he has been seeking, it comes as *something received*, as something he has *passively undergone* despite all of his active energies dispensed in seeking it.[20] What occurs in the luminous dimensions of consciousness cannot be reduced to the basic phenomenological distinction between focal and marginal awareness. It is not as if the person who seeks an insight and has all of the necessary data in front of him is focally aware of the data and only marginally aware of the insight into it. The insight itself, like poetic inspiration, cannot be an intended object. It can be neither focally nor marginally intended.

Phenomenology neglects to make this precise distinction—between the intentional and luminous dimensions of consciousness—in its treatment of historical questions. According to the standard phenomenological definition, history is "an identity in a manifold." What this means is that historical events are experienced in fundamentally different ways. Those who actively participated in them; these same people when they remember the event; those who read about it in the newspaper; those who write and read books about it later on; those who see films taken of the event; and those who see movies and television shows made about it. All intend it differently.[21] Though Voegelin admits history is an identity-in-a-manifold in this sense, he would argue it is much more still. It involves the conscious participation in an all-encompassing context that we not only act upon and observe, but that *acts upon us*, rendering us *passive recipients* just as much as conscious observers. As I indicated earlier when I distinguished between tradition-bound history and history as a horizon of mystery, there is an element of *inheritance* involved in every conscious awareness of an historical event that affects how we perceive it and act upon it. The notion of history as an encompassing context in which we participate can never be reduced to an object of intentional consciousness. This dimension of history forever eludes our mastery.

In Voegelin's later terminology, worked out most fully in *In Search of Order*, he calls this more encompassing history "It-Reality." "It" refers to that mysterious element of human grammar that surfaces when humans articulate phrases like "It is nice out" or "It is going to be a wonderful day." This strange grammatical subject reveals the paradoxical nature of human consciousness and the reality in which it participates. On one side, consciousness is something concretely located in a body—with all of its concomitant layers, from the physical and chemical, to the biological and psychological. In relation to this concretely embodied consciousness, reality appears as a series of intended objects, to which I can assign names or concepts. Voegelin terms this aspect of consciousness "Thing-reality," and its corresponding mode of consciousness is Husserlian intentionality. On the other side, we must remember that this concretely embodied consciousness does not mark the absolute beginning of reality, that reality, in its historical, societal, and cultural dimensions, *encompasses* this concrete consciousness in a way that precludes its ever being mastered entirely. In this second sense, reality is not an object of consciousness but *the something in which* consciousness occurs as an event of participation between partners in the community of being.[22] Reality, thus, changes from the position of an intended object to that of a subject, while the consciousness of the human subject intending objects moves to the position of a predicate of the subject "reality." This "paradox of consciousness" consists of the fact that the human experience of reality is marked *both* by intentionality—with its corresponding "thing-reality"—and luminosity—with its corresponding "It-reality." Consciousness exists in a state of tension between these two modes of participation in reality. In the words of Robert McMahon, "Intentionality and luminosity are polar opposites, paradoxically copresent in all experience."[23] With an action as simple as writing on a computer, one's experience is *simultaneously* luminous and intentional. One intends the computer while at the same time remaining luminously aware of the context in which one intends it. Further, one is luminously aware of the context of this context, and the ultimate context of the whole of Being. Given different types of experience, its degree of luminosity and intentionality will vary in an inverse relationship. Obviously, the mode of intentionality will be stronger, and luminosity weaker, in the experience of writing on a computer. But the opposite will be the case in, for example, the experience of a sunset. Though one does intend the sunset as an object, one is more likely in this case to *passively* let the experience affect one's psychic disposition. One "soaks it all in," so to speak, simply letting the experience overcome one's active focus on the object. Consciousness exists "in between" the two dimensions, in what Plato called the *"metaxy."* When "it" refers to some mysterious subject of a sentence that cannot be identified with any "thing" in the external world, the paradox of the *metaxy* appears most fully. The subject "it" in the sentence "it is a wonderful day" exists nowhere, and only seems to provide an index for the more encompassing reality that is the "world" in which we live.[24]

Clarity on this distinction allows us now to understand Voegelin's analysis of inner time-consciousness. According to the phenomenological method, we must distinguish between three different "levels" of temporality. There is, first, "World time" or "objective time"—that is, the measurable time of clocks and calendars, the time that belongs to worldly processes and events. Secondly, there is "internal" or "subjective" time, which belongs to the duration and sequence of mental acts and experiences, the events of conscious life. Finally, and most importantly, there is the level of our *consciousness of internal time*. This final level, in phenomenology, is the absolute level, since it functions as the domain in which the beginning of things as phenomena is achieved. As Sokolowski maintains, this level "founds everything else, but is not founded on anything."[25] As a condition for the appearance of internal time, the third level is also the condition for the appearing of the world in the "flow" or "stream" of consciousness. Objects in the world persist through the flow of time. As I experience them in the "living present," I am also simultaneously anticipating future perceptions and remembering past ones. To use the language of phenomenology, protention, retention, and the primal impression are all moments—that is, nonisolatable, nonindependent elements—of our inner time consciousness.

Yet for Voegelin, there can be no "stream" or "flow" of consciousness except by turning to a specific process of selected, simple perception—in most cases, auditory or bodily perception. A time-consciousness without an object-consciousness is difficult to describe. This difficulty can be seen in the fact that almost all analysts of time-consciousness favor the model of a perception of a tone that is heard and continues to be heard, while the beginning of the tone slides into the past but is still continuously remembered. This example shows that what is described in the event of an auditory perception is not the consciousness of time but our consciousness of our perception of the tone.[26] In other words, by directing our attention to a sound that lasts several moments, and trying to pay attention to the way in which one perceives this, one is not necessarily becoming conscious of "time" *per se*, but rather one's faculty of auditory perception and the manner in which it operates. The structure of man's faculty of perception determines the objective structure of the tone.

Voegelin sheds light on his intent when he points out that phenomenologists have never tried to describe time-consciousness on the model of a person examining a painting. Unlike a tone or a song, it is impossible to understand a painting by simultaneously staring at it and turning one's attention to the flow of time. The problems of subject, composition, color, and technique will captivate one's attention entirely, and have very little to do with time-flow. Voegelin notes, "In this process, in which the 'meaning' of the painting is constituted, time 'flows' without being noticed."[27] Of course, one can very easily extricate one's attention from the meaning of the painting so as to concentrate on the flow of one's perception. Yet, the more one succeeds in becoming conscious of perception as a time-process, the more perception begins to turn away from the colors, composition, and so on, toward others unrelated to the painting *per se*. The latter would be clearly better suited to make one conscious of the "flow" than visual perceptions. Physical perceptions like the pressure of one's feet on the floor, one's heartbeat, or breathing rhythm would probably replace the perception of the painting. Based on these experiences, Voegelin determines that time-consciousness has a specific affinity to the sphere of the senses, especially to those of the body and acoustics.[28]

   The selection of sensory perception as a model for understanding
time-consciousness is not, for Voegelin, the best way to understand the time
problem. All this perception does, in reality, is bring one's attention to the
undeniable fact that consciousness is grounded in the organic body and that it
cannot truly exist apart from it.[29] To say that one experiences "time" in these
examples would be to engage in a speculative construction. The reason why
so many reputable philosophers have entertained this approach is because
the "flow" as such—the gliding and sliding away, the primal impression,
protention, and retention—is so fascinating, as it reveals the "fleetingness"
of our sensory awareness. "But," Voegelin continues, "the selection of this
class of experiences seems to reveal that one must *rely on the sphere of the
senses* in order to make us conscious of the 'fleetingness' of consciousness,
in which, by the way, not everything is fleeting."[30] This class of experiences
is theoretically important to the extent that it makes us aware of the intimate
connection between consciousness and the body. But it does not exhaust the
dimensions of consciousness. The experience of "flow," as demonstrated in
the tone model, is only possible if one turns one's attention to it. The "flow"
does not generate the consciousness of time. Instead, consciousness, *which
itself is not flowing*, generates the experience of flow. Voegelin concludes that
consciousness and its structures, whatever they may be, are *given antecedents*
to any and all experiences of "flow."[31]

   For Husserl, and phenomenology generally, that element of consciousness that does not flow is the transcendental "I," acting as the basis for the
third level of time-consciousness, the *consciousness of* inner time. This "I"
constitutes our experience of the world, which is not possible apart from it.
Yet Voegelin sees a problem with this approach. The effort to look for some
"I" that would be the agent constituting this flow is also misguided and still
affected by the human proclivity to view its experiences under the model of
intentionality. As opposed to Husserl, Voegelin wants to understand the "I" as
a phenomenon *within* consciousness rather than as the form of consciousness
itself. In this regard, he acknowledges some of the breakthroughs in Freud's
psychoanalytic investigations. Freud, more than Husserl, saw fundamental
givens of psychic life clearly. To him, the "I" is rather a highly complex *symbol* for certain directional determinants within consciousness.[32] Voegelin and
Freud, unlike Husserl, make the crucial distinction between the *experience*
to which the symbol "I" is attributed and the *symbol itself*. To illustrate this
point, Voegelin describes the act of getting up from a chair:

> I "will" to get up from my chair and observe how the "willing" and the "getting
> up" proceed. I can clearly recognize the project of my "getting up," but what
> occurs between my decision and my actual getting up remains quite obscure. I
> do not know why I get up just at this moment and not a second later. As closely

as I may observe the process, all I can find is that at the actual getting up something, from a source inaccessible to me, makes me get up and that nothing of an "I" is discoverable in the act. This observation does not tell me anything about the determinacy or indeterminacy of acting; it merely indicates that the actual getting up does not occur in the form of "I".[33]

The phenomenon of "attentiveness" also shows that consciousness seems to have an *energy center*—though not a hypostatized "I"—whose force varies between individuals and even within the same individual depending upon the time of the day. This "energy center" can be directed to different dimensions of consciousness, such as the past, present, or future. It is important to emphasize that these acts of concentration stem not from the "I"—which functions merely as a linguistic index or symbol—but from some "inner illumination"—some center of energy—which is engaged in a process that cannot be observed from without, as one can observe the movements of objects or "things" of the external world.[34] One observes the motions of objects—such as a clock ticking or a car driving past—in a different mode than one experiences this inner illumination, which cannot be "observed" at all. "One must," according to Voegelin, "avoid the misconception that the dimensions of consciousness are something like empty slates on which data can be entered, the misconception that there is something like a time problem 'as such,' apart from the process of a substance."[35] Hegel, Husserl, and other end of history speculators attempt to do precisely this: they look upon time as if it were external to the inner illumination of consciousness, a "thing" bound up with the things of the external world. This distortion of the reality of time can be seen most clearly in the almost universal human tendency to conceive of history as a timeline on which events can be placed, as if there were "time slots" in which data can be entered. One thereby conceives of the past and future in spatial thing-like dimensions.[36]

As an alternative to this distortion, Voegelin suggests we understand past and future as the "present illuminative dimensions of the process in which the energy center is engaged."[37] While he admits this description is just as much a symbolism as any, its main features gain a higher level of differentiation. Through the illuminative dimensions of past and future, one becomes aware of the structures of a *finite process* between birth and death, not empty spaces on an external timeline. The experience of consciousness is the experience of a process, and this is the only process we know "from within." Voegelin continues: "Because of this characteristic quality, the process of consciousness becomes the model of the process as such, the only experiential model to serve as the orientation point of the conceptual apparatus *through which we must also grasp the processes that transcend consciousness*."[38] The process of consciousness "from within" almost inevitably—though not justifiably—becomes the model for understanding processes "from without," such as the process of history or time per se. Though we cannot avoid it, since the inner illumination of the past and future dimensions of consciousness are really all we have as models, the "infinite" processes of time and history cannot and should not be taken literally under the model of the "finite" processes of consciousness. We have no experience of infinite processes "as a whole." That is, we cannot experience time and history "as wholes" in the same way we can experience an object or creature in the external world, whose developmental stages can be observed closely and documented. We cannot really say that time and history have a beginning or an end because we have no experience of an ultimate beginning "in time." The only time of which we do have experience is the inner experience of the illuminated dimensions of consciousness, "the process that drops away, at both ends, past and future, into unilluminated darkness."[39]

The chief problem with all end of history speculations is that they try to understand history as a "whole," as if finite consciousness could somehow wrap itself around an infinite process. In order to accomplish this feat, they select a single line of meaning in this process and use it to posit an absolute beginning and an absolute end to the process. Humans can say there is a *telos* in creaturely life because it is possible to watch organisms as they are born, develop, mature, decline, and die. The *entirety* of the process is there to be discovered. In contrast, no currently living human being was present at the beginning of history, since it extends into a necessarily obscure past. Likewise, no human being has been present at the end of history, since it keeps developing in new and unforeseen ways into an indefinite future, unleashing ever new possibilities and potential.

Human beings have learned to cope with the inevitable uncertainties of past and future—while at the same time preserving their mystery—through mythological symbolism. As we saw in a previous chapter, historiogenesis often takes the form of mytho-speculation on the origins of humans (anthropogony), Gods (theogony), and the cosmos (cosmogony). These myths enable us to *finitize a transfinite process*. A mythical symbol is a finite symbol intended to provide "transparence" for a transfinite process.[40] Since the processes that transcend consciousness—such as history itself—are not internally experienceable, we have no other means of characterizing their structure except through symbols derived from finite experiences. Consequently, anthropomorphic images of God and creation stories—meant to make experience of transcendence "transparent" are a structural constant in the historical process. These stories and symbolisms do *not* provide closure to the mysteries they symbolize. Instead, *they facilitate the experience of mystery*. If understood correctly, myths are supposed to "open" one up to the mysteries of the various transfinite processes. Unlike the end of history speculations, they are not meant to provide certainty, but can only act as guides by means of which one can meditatively experience the deep mystery of reality.

The preceding reflections crystallize in Voegelin's concluding statement:

> There is no absolute beginning for a philosophy of consciousness. All philosophizing about consciousness is an event (*Ereignis*) in the consciousness of the philosopher and presupposes this consciousness together with its structures. Inasmuch as the consciousness of philosophizing is not "pure" consciousness, but rather the consciousness of a human being, all philosophizing is an event in the philosopher's life history; an event in the history of the community with its symbolic language; an event in the history of mankind; and an event in the history of the cosmos. No "human" in his reflection on consciousness and its nature can make consciousness an "object" to be confronted; the reflection is rather an orientation within consciousness with which he can push to its limits but never cross them. Consciousness is a given in the elemental sense that systematic reflection on consciousness is a late event in the biography of a philosopher. The philosopher always lives in the context of his own history, the history of a human existence in the community and in the world.[41]

Philosophy is not something that arises immediately in the life of an individual. Usually, it happens late in an individual's life due to some crisis or question forced upon him. It is an "event" in the course of several more encompassing histories, including the individual's unique life-history, the history of the society in which he lives, the history of the world, and the history of the cosmos. Because the latter three histories encompass the individual's life—in fact, form the necessary preconditions for it—it is impossible for an individual to step outside the historical process to contemplate it as a whole. He has a necessarily limited perspective that can only delude itself into the position of a subject standing over against an historical object with an essence and *telos*.

To summarize: history is not and can never be an "object" about which speculation is possible. What the historian does is *participate* in the more encompassing history about which he is writing. The writing of history, therefore, has the dual significance of being both a speculation about meaning and a participation in it. The historiographer's work is part of what Voegelin in "What Is History?" calls the "expressive surface" of history. That is to say, it is both the *result* of history and *an act which constitutes* history. The subject-object dichotomy, which is part of the phenomenal surface of this same history, is a secondary stratum within this primary expressive surface.[42] We, as concretely existing human beings depending on our environments and physiology to stay alive, experience reality in both the modes of "thing-reality" and "it-reality," and it is the paradox or tension that arises from this bifocal experience that forms the core of the human condition.

NOTES

1. Much has been written about Voegelin's philosophy of consciousness, but few scholars have explored the relationship between it and Voegelin's Philosophy of History. Robert McMahon, for instance, in "Voegelin's Paradoxes of Consciousness" gives an extremely lucid and thought-provoking analysis of some of Voegelin's key conceptual tools for understanding human consciousness, such as "thing-reality" and "it-reality," the meaning of the term "participant," and "luminosity" and "intentionality." Yet this article says very little about the relationship between historiography and the terms it clarifies. Though this article is essential reading for anybody looking to better understand this "key to all" of Voegelin's works, it ultimately fails to show its thesis' simplications for Voegelin's critique of the stop-history movements—something which I aim to do in this chapter.

2. Eric Voegelin, *New Science of Politics*, 1.

3. Eric Voegelin, *Anamnesis* (Columbia: University of Missouri Press, 1990), 33. In the opening lines of this work, Voegelin states, "The problems of human order in society and history originate in the order of consciousness. Hence the philosophy of consciousness is the centerpiece of a philosophy of politics." This marks a complete reversal of the principles laid out in the opening lines of *The New Science of Politics*.

4. Though I will show in what follows that Voegelin's relationship to Intentionality analysis is ambiguous, complex, and ultimately negative, this has not prevented some Voegelin scholars from drawing a clear link between it and Voegelin's philosophy. Michael Federici, for instance, in *Eric Voegelin: The Restoration of Order* (Wilmington: ISI Books, 2002), states, "Voegelin uses Husserl's concept of 'intentionality' to refer to the relation between human consciousness and reality. Consciousness, according to Voegelin, is consciousness of reality, that is, consciousness intends reality as its object" (137). Contrary to this statement, Voegelin's philosophy of consciousness, I will argue, does not fully embrace intentionality, but rather views it as merely applicable to certain realms of being which must be contextualized within a more comprehensive understanding of human consciousness. The term Voegelin uses to label this more comprehensive understanding of human consciousness is "luminosity."

5. Voegelin, *Anamnesis*, 33.

6. The orientation of Husserl's theory toward the model of immanent objects in the external world shows that he has gnostic tendencies. In the words of Mark T. Mitchell in "Michael Polanyi, Eric Voegelin, and the Indispensability of Faith," "Gnosticism is an attempt to circumvent the ontological and epistemological uncertainty of the life of faith by attempting to alter the fundamental structure of reality better to produce certainty. This can only be accomplished by bringing the meaning of existence into the purview of human control: the transcendent truth of reality must be immanentized" (74).

7. Robert Sokolowski, *Introduction to Phenomenology* (New York: Cambridge University Press, 2000), 8.

8. Voegelin, *Anamnesis*, 43.

9. Ibid., 46.

10. Ibid.

11. Ibid., 47.

12. Ibid., 47.

13. Edmund Husserl, *Crisis of the European Sciences and Transcendental Phenomenology* (Evanston: Northwestern University Press, 1970), 71.

14. Ibid., 51.

15. Ibid., 15.

16. Ibid., 16.

17. Voegelin, *Anamnesis*, 51–52.

18. Ibid., 54.

19. Robert McMahon, "Eric Voegelin's Paradoxes of Consciousness and Participation," 120.

20. Cf. Bernard Lonergan's analysis of an insight in *Insight* (Toronto: University of Toronto Press, 1992), 28–30. There is much compatibility between Lonergan's study of intellectual insight and Voegelin's analysis of the luminous dimensions of consciousness.

21. Sokolowski, *Introduction to Phenomenology*, 29.

22. Eric Voegelin, *In Search of Order* (Columbia: University of MIssouri Press, 2000), 29.

23. Robert McMahon, "Voegelin's Paradoxes of Consciousness and Participation," The Review of Politics 61, no. 1 (Winter, 1999) 119.

24. McMahon notes that Voegelin discovered this paradox of consciousness through his opposition to Hegel, who when faced with the paradoxic structure of language and reality, tried to invent his own metalanguage that would "out-comprehend the comprehending reality" ("Voegelin's Paradoxes," 130. I disagree with this statement. As I will show later, Hegel's insight into the paradoxic structure of reality has to do precisely with how the Idea has proceeded and will continue to proceed in the historical course. Hegel's claim to Absolute knowledge is nothing more and nothing less than the articulation of the conditions for the supersession of his system.

25. Sokolowski, *Introduction to Phenomenology*, 131.

26. Voegelin, *Anamnesis*, 63.

27. Ibid.

28. Ibid., 64.

29. Ibid., 65.

30. Ibid., 64.

31. Ibid., 65–66.

32. Ibid., 67. As Husserl of course acknowledges, this would be to attempt to view the "I" as an object. For Husserl, as for Voegelin, the "I," or as Voegelin will call it "the energy center," can never be an object of intentional consciousness.

33. Ibid., 67.

34. One could object that Voegelin has simply changed the name of a nonhypostatized "I" to "energy center" without really changing the phenomena underlying them in any way. This objection appears legitimate. However, it may be the case that Voegelin made this change deliberately as a result of some of the illegitimate baggage

that has accrued to the symbol "I" over the years. If this is true, Voegelin perhaps thought that "energy center" was a more accurate symbol for its designation.

35. Ibid., 68.

36. Voegelin is here influenced by Henri Bergson's analysis of the time problem and his treatment of "*durée.*" See Henri Bergson, *The Creative Mind: An Introduction to Metaphysics* (Mineola: Dover Publications, 2007), 1–17.

37. Ibid., 68.

38. Ibid., 69. My emphasis.

39. Ibid., 69. Voegelin compares his analysis to Kant's antinomies of infinity, and the paradoxes that result. The causal series cannot begin in time because we have no experience of a beginning "in time." More precisely, one could say that we have no experience whatsoever of a time in which something might begin.

40. Ibid., 69.

41. Ibid., 81.

42. "What Is History?" in *What Is History? and Other Late Unpublished Writings*, ed. Thomas Hollweck and Paul Caringella (Columbia: University of Missouri Press, 1990) 12.

Chapter 9

Kojève's Hegel on
Time and History

Among the most important points I have argued in this section is that, in Voegelin's eyes, Hegel's distortion of history results from a theoretical mistake of viewing history in the mode of intentionality, as an object that can be taken in as a whole in its phenomenological dimensions. But besides the fact that his most famous work is entitled a "phenomenology," Hegel has no explicit relationship to Husserl. Indeed, Husserl writes almost a hundred years after Hegel, and while Hegel's influence upon Husserl is evident, it is simply chronologically impossible that Husserl could have had an influence upon Hegel. So, on the basis of what, then, does Voegelin stake this claim? In what follows, I will attempt to show that Kojève's lectures on Hegel's *Phenomenology of Spirit* suggested a link between Hegel's views on time and history and intentional consciousness.

From the outset, we can remark that Kojève expressly states in the *Remarques Préliminaires* of his *Introduction* that Hegel's *Phenomenology* is a phenomenology in the Husserlian sense: "The *Phenomenology* is a phenomenological description (*in the Husserlian sense of the word*); its 'object' is man inasmuch as he is an 'existential phenomenon'; man such as he appears (*erscheint*) to himself in and by his existence. And the *Phenomenology* itself is his last appearance."[1] The *Phenomenology of Spirit*, thus, in Kojève's understanding, consists of a subject (Hegel) standing over against an object (the history of mankind in all of its political, cultural, religious, and existential dimensions). The purpose of the book is for this subject to conceptually absorb this object—that is, to comprehend it completely and articulate its meaning. There is to be an "identity-in-difference" between this subject and this object, such that the one will be indistinguishable from the other. This complete conceptual penetration can only occur after the historical/temporal course has been completed. Indeed, this conceptual penetration actually *marks the completion* of this course.

In his "Note sur l'éternité, le temps, et le Concept" (Note on Eternity, Time, and the Concept), Kojève describes the ontological mechanics of this course in much more detail. By contrasting Hegel's views on the relationship between Time, Eternity, and the Concept with those of Plato, Parmenides, Spinoza, Aristotle, and Kant, he aims to demonstrate that Hegel resolves all of the inevitable conceptual contradictions these other philosophers could articulate but not overcome. The contradictions reveal the very complicated manner in which Time—or, rather, the unfolding of the historical process—relates to the Concept—for example, the logical/conceptual articulation of truth. To summarize these contradictions: first, Parmenides and Spinoza identify the Concept with Eternity. That is to say that, for them, the Concept—the logical structure of the universe, the "thoughts of God before creation"—has no relation to Time. Absolute Knowing, as the complete conceptual penetration of this structure, is therefore only a possibility outside of Time, completely removed from flux and change. Due to this identification, the temporal existence of the Concept in the world is inexplicable from Parmenides's and Spinoza's point of view.[2] It would be impossible for humans, who live in time and thus are subject to change and flux, to access the Concept in any way. But this would then seem to contradict their claims to have discovered this same Concept. The Parmenido-Spinozist position ends therefore in a paradox.

An alternative is Plato's position, which claims the existence of man (in Time) is necessary for knowledge. True knowledge—that is, the Concept—is now a relation between two necessary elements, "*l'homme* (man)," situated in empirical existence in Time, and "*l'Eternité* (Eternity)," situated outside of Time, *hors du Temps*. Of course, the "eternal" is different from "Eternity." The knowledge men can achieve is eternal, and thus has a relation to Eternity, but it is not fully Eternity, the Concept outside of time. The eternal Concept—not to be confused with the Concept completely outside of Time—is much closer to Time than the "parménido-spinoziste" Concept. But not being Eternity, it still relates to Eternity, and the Eternity to which it relates has nothing to do with Time.[3] Plato's philosophy thus presents us with another contradiction.

Aristotle is the first one to say that Time itself penetrates into Absolute Knowledge. The Eternity to which the eternal Concept relates is now situated *in time*. However, Time only enters into Absolute Knowledge to the extent that Time itself is eternal. This is the reason why Aristotle must posit the "eternal return" of the same. Kant, the only other modern author Kojève discusses, is the first to break with the Aristotelian pagan conception and to take account of the Judeo-Christian anthropology according to which man is a historical being. For Kant, the Concept—while remaining eternal—relates to Time as Time. But for him, Time and the Concept remain a priori forms of intuition, only hypothetically having any relation to the thing-in-itself. Kant's position, thus, boils down to a declaration that attaining Absolute Knowing is impossible.

What Hegel does is *fully* identify Time and the Concept. In other words, he completely eliminates the need for a transcendent basis for our eternal knowledge. This identification distinguishes him from all of his philosophical predecessors. There is no longer a *Ding-an-sich* (thing-in-itself) off limits to human knowledge. Time *is* the Concept. The latter can *only* unfold temporally. Time is the Concept itself existing *empirically*. For Kojève, the basic fault of all Hegel's philosophical predecessors is that they cannot fully account for the *fact of history*. Man, in his essence, is a historical creature, a free creature, subject to desires and capable of acting on them, a creature able to change his essence and that of the world in which he lives. As Kojève states,

> On a phenomenological level, the philosophy (or, more precisely, the "science") of Hegel describes the existence of man who sees himself living in a world where he knows himself to be a free and historical individual. On a metaphysical level, this philosophy tells us what a world in which man can appear in this way must be like. Finally, on an ontological level it is a matter of seeing what Being itself must be like to be able to exist with such a world. And Hegel responds by saying that this is only possible if the real Concept (that is to say, Being itself revealed to itself by an empirically existing Discourse) is Time.[4]

Otherwise stated, Hegel's scientific project is an attempt to lay out the complete set of interlocking conditions—metaphysical, ontological, physical, historical, political, religious, and cultural—for the emergence of a fully rational and free existence.[5] The *Phenomenology of Spirit* describes phenomenologically the course of Spirit as it makes its way through history to arrive at the point at which it can articulate these conditions. The Concept, which we later find out is also identified with Spirit, must be identified with Time for this to be possible.

To reiterate, the Time he identifies with the Concept is first and foremost *historical time.* Hegel, according to Kojève, is not talking about the movements of the sun and moon and stars. Time, for him, is not "natural" Time understood and measured by means of these celestial bodies. Rather, the only real Time is the Time in which human history unfolds, the Time that actualizes itself as a Universal History. There is only Time to the extent that there is history, and there is only history to the extent that there are human beings—that is, *speaking beings who are rational and free.* The man who, over the course of history, reveals Being through his Logos (speech/word), is the *empirically existing* Concept (*der daseiende Begriff*), and Time is nothing else than this Concept.[6] Time, therefore, would not exist without the presence of human beings. According to Kojève's Hegel, Man is Time and Time is Man—the Concept that is there (*là*) in empirical existence (*l'existence-empirique*).

What inaugurates History—and thus Time, understood in this Hegelian-Kojèvian sense—is the appearance of the most fundamental human desire—namely, the desire for universal recognition (*la Reconnaissance Universelle*). Before this desire emerged in consciousness, human beings were no more than animals whose needs and desires never went beyond the basic biological necessities of food, sex, water, and shelter that are needed for survival. Human beings are unique, however, insomuch as they can forgo these biological necessities for higher purposes. As Hegel demonstrates by means of the Master-Slave dialectic, they are willing to sacrifice their lives to satiate this desire for recognition. All truly historical acts and events can be traced back to this primordial desire, according to Kojève. All properly human and historical acts are accomplished with a view to this social recognition. The dialectics of Time and History thus begin when this desire first emerges, and end when this desire is completely satisfied. As mentioned earlier, the advent of the Universal and Homogeneous State accomplishes this historical mission.[7]

Time is present in the world as the Desire for Universal Recognition. The need to annihilate the world (*néantissement du monde*)—in its politically, ethically, and culturally instantiated institutions—until it conforms to this primordial desire is the most fundamental historical fact. One can, in Kojève's Hegel's view, understand the *meaning of the whole historical course* if one recognizes this one fact. Over the course of history, we witness nothing but change and destruction, as no society prior to the Universal and Homogeneous State was able to recognize all human beings. Some recognized specific populations of people—say, Greeks, Christians, Whites, or Han—but this recognition was not universal. By making this discovery and incorporating it into a fully worked-out system of knowledge, Hegel has conceptually penetrated the transcendent mystery that had hitherto shrouded the unfolding of history. History and Time are thus reduced to the dialectical working-out of this *world-immanent* desire. "Time," as Kojève states, "is an X, a some-*thing* (*un quelque chose*), that exists *empirically* (qui existe empiriquement)."[8] This "thing" is the empirically existing human desire that negates the external world until it conforms to the primordial desire. The historical course can thus be condensed as follows:

> Man is desire carried toward another desire; that is, the desire for recognition; that is, the negating action carried out with a view toward satisfying this desire for recognition; that is, the bloody battle for prestige; that is, the relationship between master and slave; that is, labor; that is, the historical evolution that

finally arrives at the Universal and Homogeneous State and at the Absolute Knowledge that reveals the integral man realized in and by this State.[9]

This passage encapsulates the meaning and general contours of Kojève's Universal History. The need for a transcendent basis of meaning—understood in the sense of It-Reality, a nonreducible cosmic unfolding that encompasses each particular human society and each individual within each human society—is nonexistent in this Kojèvian-Hegelian explanation for the historical course. This world-immanent desire for recognition is the highest human aspiration, and therefore any discussion of meaning derived from a divine "beyond" transcending this immanent historical course is invalid or irrelevant from the get-go. Man can and will be *completely satisfied* when the Universal and Homogeneous State succeeds in granting this universal recognition. Time and History will end. The Concept will be completely actualized.

In Kojève's reading of the *Phenomenology of Spirit*, man and the historical course of which he is a part are reduced to objects conforming to the mode of speculation of "Thing-Reality." In this sense, man's consciousness is nothing but various world-immanent appetites and desires, the most important of which is the desire for universal recognition. It is only by reducing human beings to objects in "Thing-Reality" that Kojève is able to pronounce definitively on the meaning and purpose of their lives. Furthermore, by identifying Time with the Concept, Kojève does away completely with the human orientation toward transcendent being. There are no longer aspects of the Concept off limits to finite human beings. Time is nothing but the negation of the natural and human worlds until they completely conform to fully actualized Spirit in the Universal and Homogeneous State.

NOTES

1. Alexandre Kojève, *Introduction à la lecture de Hegel*, ed. Raymond Queneau (Mesnil-sur-l'Estrée: Gallimard, 2001), 38. My translation from the French: "La Phénoménologie est une description phénoménologique (au sens husserlien du mot); son 'objet,' c'est l'homme en tant que 'phénomène existentiel'; l'homme tel qu'il apparaît (erscheint) à lui-même dans son existence et par elle. Et la Phénoménologie elle-même est sa dernière apparition."

2. Ibid., 364.

3. Ibid.

4. Ibid., 365. My translation from the French: "Sur son plan phénoménologique, la philosophie (ou plus exactement, la 'science') de Hegel décrit l'existence de l'Homme qui se voit vivre dans un Monde où il se sait être un individu libre et historique. Et dans son plan métaphysique, cette philosophie nous dit quel doit être le Monde où l'Homme peut s'apparaître ainsi. Enfin, dans le plan ontologique, il s'agit de voir

quel doit être l'Être lui-même pour pouvoir exister en tant qu'un tel Monde. Et Hegel répond en disant que ceci n'est possible que si le Concept réel (c'est-à-dire l'Être révélé lui-même à lui-même par un Discours existant empiriquement) est Temps."

5. Because of this fact, some might argue that Hegel does indeed acknowledge some sort of encompassing "It-Reality" which conditions our lives. While this is true, it must be emphasized that, at least in Kojève's reading, Hegel's articulation of the interlocking set of conditions for rational and free existence is *complete* and *absolute*. So while other individuals may still be conditioned or determined by them, Hegel himself is "absolved" from them—that is, he has become completely free from the encompassing "It-reality" in and through his complete articulation of it.

6. Kojève, *Introduction*, 366.

7. Ibid., 368.

8. Ibid., 369.

9. Ibid., 371. My translation from the French: "L'homme est Désir portant sur un autre Désir; c'est-à-dire Désir de Reconnaissance; c'est-à-dire Action négatrice effectuée en vue de satisfaire ce Désir de Reconnaissance; c'est-à-dire Lutte sanglante de prestige; c'est-à-dire rapport entre Maître et Esclave; c'est-à-dire Travail; c'est-à-dire évolution historique qui arrive finalement à l'Etat universel et homogène et au Savoir absolu qui révèle l'Homme intégral réalisé dans et par cet Etat."

Chapter 10

Voegelin on the Problem of Time and the "Stop-History" Movements

It bears repeating that Voegelin's estimation of Time and History differs considerably from Kojève's. As we saw, one of the unquestioned presuppositions of the Kojèvian position is that man's most fundamental desire is for Universal Recognition, and it is this desire that inaugurates Time and History properly understood. In order to have a hermetically sealed system, along with the illusion that this system is complete and final, this presupposition must remain unquestioned. Voegelin stresses the unwillingness to discuss presuppositions as a mark of an ideological thinker: "These 'stop-history' systems that dominate the contemporary scene can maintain the appearance of truth only by an act of violence, for example, by prohibiting questions concerning the premises and by making the prohibition a formal part of the System."[1] The Kojèvian pronouncement that the meaning of history is the working-out of human freedom and universal recognition is thus, in Voegelin's view, somewhat arbitrary. This does not mean the desire for recognition isn't manifest at all in history, for it is possible that many human actions and historical events are motivated by it. Yet to make the claim that this desire is the *highest* and *most uniquely human*, or that a political order like the universal and homogeneous state will *completely* satisfy man's spiritual longings, would be to overlook other important dimensions of the human soul that *cannot be completely satisfied* with world-immanent reality. The "Question" at the heart of human existence—that is, the Question about the primordial mystery of the meaning of the cosmos—remains to disrupt any and all attempts to pronounce definitively about this meaning. It ensures that history will continue in new and unprecedented ways, as humans continue to strive for a transcendent purpose that constantly eludes their grasp.

Instead of responding to the Question in a way that would preserve the meaning of history as the horizon of divine mystery, Kojève and other "stop-history" speculators engage in a profound distortion of the meaning of Time. As we saw, Kojève's Hegel looked upon Time and History as empirically existing things that must run their course for a certain length of time before they have supplied the material past on which a thinker can base "scientific" propositions concerning the order that governs the process.[2] These thinkers attempt to solve historical issues belonging to the "in-between" reality of divine-human participation by conceiving of time in the mode of Thing-reality as a world-immanent process. In contrast, Voegelin states that there is no such thing as a "length of time" in which historical events happen. Rather, time is conceived as a *mode of lasting* in the divine-human in-between of historically differentiating experience founded in the consciousness of concrete human beings in concrete bodies on the concrete earth in the concrete universe. There is only the reality of things that have a time dimension. Time itself cannot be understood as a thing.[3]

In formulating a theory of time, Voegelin takes into account the "mode of lastingness" of the various strata or levels of Being, beginning with the inorganic stratum, through the vegetative and animal realms, to the existence of man in his tension toward the divine ground. Man consists of all of these strata. The lower form the conditions and foundations for the higher, and these in turn act as the organizing principle for the lower. Man could not exist without the physical laws of the universe that ground the chemical laws upon which metabolic bodily processes depend. The metabolic bodily processes, in turn, act as the conditions that allow for the possibility of physiologically healthy lives, and thus ground man's higher-order intellectual and emotional activities, such as the desire for social recognition (Kojève) and the desire for transcendent purpose (Voegelin). There is, thus, a process of the Whole, of which these various strata and the historical process are parts. As Voegelin remarks,

> Within this process of the Whole, then, some things, as for instance the earth, outlast other things, as for instance the individual human beings who inhabit the earth; and what we call "time" without further qualifications is the mode of lastingness peculiar to the astrophysical universe that permits its dimension of time to be measured by its movements in space. But even this ultimate mode of lastingness, to which as a measure we refer the lasting of all other things, is not a "time" in which things happen but the time dimension of a thing within the Whole that also comprises the divine reality whose mode of lastingness we express by such symbols as "eternity." Things do not happen in the astrophysical universe; the universe, together with all things founded in it, happens in God.[4]

What we usually call "time" is more often than not a hypostasized way of measuring the lastingness of some object of the astrophysical universe in comparison to another. This mode of measuring the lastingness of objects is not at all dangerous, so long as one remains aware that one has not exhausted the meaning of time. One of the most common distortions of time is the use of a "time-line" to conceptually order events. This way of conceiving of the time-process predisposes us to misunderstand its true nature, as we come to look at it as a hypostasized "course" with a beginning and end, with significant events falling somewhere in between. The phenomenon of the timeline is a way for the human mind to form an imaginative representation of an unimaginable reality. As with any imagined or physically represented line, one must arbitrarily decide where the line begins and where it ends. The "Stop-History" System builders find this way of conceiving of time convenient for this reason. They can choose, according to their individual preferences, just where the "line" of history begins—in Kojève's case with the emergence of the desire for recognition—and, accordingly, where it will end—presumably with the resolution of the conflict which inaugurates the historical process.

In consequence, it is clear that Voegelin's earliest reflections on consciousness and the limitations of Husserlian phenomenology still have far-reaching implications for a philosophy of history. These later, more mature, reflections on the nature of Time permit us to see the abiding significance of a philosophy of consciousness that does justice to the dimensions of consciousness other than those of thing-reality. Consciousness has structures and experiences that are not reducible to objects in the external world. Time and History are part of It-reality, and we must beware the perennial temptation to view them in the mode of thing-reality. One major aspect of Voegelin's critique of end of history speculators can be summarized as follows: individuals like Kojève and Hegel falsely assume—either due to carelessness, spiritual depravity, or sheer ignorance—that Time unfolds as a "line." For this reason, it can be viewed as a "whole" as soon as enough time has elapsed. The only way to determine whether enough time has elapsed is to arbitrarily posit some beginning to this historical timeline. The nature of this beginning will, in turn, determine its end. In the case of Kojève, the ideals and values of a post–World War Two Universal and Homogeneous Europe provided the impetus for selecting the "Desire for Recognition" as the foundation for "history" properly understood. In a similar way, the Europe of the Napoleonic Empire influenced Hegel's selection of this same foundation. What all of the "stop-history" movements have in common is the attempt to eliminate the transcendent mystery that envelops the historical process. Because Time should be understood, not as a "line," but as the mode of lastingness of objects in the astrophysical universe, the mysterious Divine Eternity encompassing these objects—the It-Reality of

human consciousness—must not be overlooked if one is to properly understand what meaning there is in history.

NOTES

1. Eric Voegelin, *The Ecumenic Age* (Columbia: University of Missouri Press,
2000), 404.
2. Ibid., 407.
3. Ibid., 408.
4. Ibid., 408.

PART IV

Hegel's Eclipse of Reality

Chapter 11

Hegel as Psychiatric Case Study?

Many readers of Voegelin's essay "On Hegel: A Study in Sorcery" come away from it with the overwhelming impression that Voegelin has not only misunderstood Hegel but has distorted his thinking in the worst possible way. His observations seem speculative at best, silly *ad hominem* arguments hardly grounded in a close reading of any of Hegel's texts.[1] If Voegelin's intention in this essay were to understand Hegel's thought on a theoretical level, then these accusations would have some validity. However, a close reading of Voegelin's essay reveals a much different intention. This essay presents itself, not as an exegesis, interpretation, or analysis of Hegel's thinking, but as a *psychiatric case study* in which Voegelin uses then-current insights in the field of psychopathology to diagnose and understand Hegel, and all other system-builders or stop-history speculators, as someone suffering from what R. D. Laing calls "ontological insecurity."[2] Voegelin's seemingly out-of-context citations appear then in a new light, as "clinical data" used to support a psychopathological diagnosis, not evidence to support a thesis interpreting Hegel's theories. Many of Voegelin's criticisms really do amount to a series of *ad hominem* arguments, since that was precisely his intention, to go *to the man* and the fundamental experiences that made up his existence.

One of the unique aspects of Voegelin's thought was his belief that the problems with end of history speculators on a theoretical level arise from a problem with these individuals on an existential level. Hegel, like other stop-history speculators, has misunderstood history because of an *existential deficiency*. The interaction of these thinkers' "two selves"—a true self, which *correctly* diagnoses the spiritual, ethical, and intellectual diseases of the day, and a false self, which sees itself as a messiah or inaugurator of a new age—results in what Voegelin calls the "Eclipse of Reality." The Second Reality of the stop-history speculators' imaginative future eclipses First Reality, the reality of the *metaxy* in all of its anthropological, societal, cultural, and religious dimensions. This section aims to lay out the rudiments of Voegelin's diagnosis of Hegel's psychopathological state. It will show

93

that while Voegelin certainly has theoretical disagreements with Hegel and other stop-history speculators—as has been demonstrated in the previous two parts—*the very core of his critique is psychological and existential.* As odd as it may sound, Voegelin saw himself as some sort of existential clinical psychiatrist—after the likes of R. D. Laing—who expanded the horizon of clinical psychiatry beyond those deemed "insane" to include studies of *intellectuals demonstrating schizoid symptoms.* I will begin with a brief exposition of the essential theses in R. D. Laing's *The Divided Self: An Existential Study in Sanity and Madness,* the work on which Voegelin relies in his efforts to understand Hegel and other stop-history speculators. I will then show how Voegelin appropriates Laing's theories for his own purposes. Next, I will show how Voegelin relates this theory of the Divided Self to his conception of the Eclipse of Reality, specifically, First and Second realities and their correspondence with the Real Self and the Contracted or False Self.

It is important to keep in mind as I begin this analysis that I am not arguing that what Voegelin says about Hegel's existential state is necessarily accurate. In fact, in the next part of this book I will argue precisely the opposite—that Voegelin's criticisms of Hegel are more or less unfounded, relying as they do on Kojève's *Introduction.* My intention in this analysis is nothing more than to understand Voegelin's critique on its own ground so that we may provide a viable and accurate context for discussion in the next section.

NOTES

1. See, for instance, Thomas J. Altizer's review of Voegelin's critique of Hegel in "A New History and a New But Ancient God?" in *The Journal for the American Academy of Religion,* Vol. 43, No. 4 (December 1975), 757–764.

2. See Voegelin's letter of November 12, 1970, to Manfred Henningsen, in which he mentions, less than a year before the publication of "Hegel: A Study in Sorcery," that the problems he is pursuing have to do with understanding "how to eventually distinguish between clinical schizophrenia and the schism of consciousness of system constructors" (in *Selected Correspondence: 1950–1984* [Columbia: University of Missouri Press, 2007], 676.)

Chapter 12

Voegelin and R. D. Laing on the Divided Self

Voegelin's reading of *The Divided Self: An Existential Study in Sanity and Madness,* was pivotal for his mature understanding of gnostic and pneuma-pathological intellectuals. It provided him with the concepts to understand more completely the consciousness of men like Hegel who, he believed, suffered first and foremost from existential deficiencies rather than a lack of intellectual acumen. According to a letter from November 25, 1967, to Manfred Henningsen, Voegelin's initial impression of Laing's work was positive. He mentions that it "fits right into my current problems insofar as the schizoid symptoms of the contracted self have their pathological continuation in schizophrenic symptoms."[1] In another letter to Francesco Mercadante from March 21, 1969, Voegelin also touches on the peculiar applicability of Laing's theories to modern intellectuals. He suggests that the distinctive pathologies of these same intellectuals are a completely unexplored topic: "The pathology of modern reason (the illegitimate use made of the reasoning power) is an entirely unexplored field. And even more unexplored are the causes of modern pathology, or pneumapathology as Schelling has called it. The schizophrenic factor in modern thought has only quite recently come to attention, as in the work of the English psychologist Laing."[2] What becomes clear from Voegelin's correspondence immediately preceding the publication of "On Hegel: A Study in Sorcery" is that Laing's theory of the two selves—the false self and the true self—provided Voegelin with one of the hermeneutical keys he was looking for in trying to understand the spiritual depravity of his time. His previous diagnosis of modern intellectuals as "gnostic," while still valid, did not quite penetrate deep enough into the existential factors influencing and distinguishing them from ancient Gnostics.[3]

Voegelin summarizes the peculiar problem of the modern gnostic intellectual in another 1967 letter to Peter Leuschner:

95

The main problem was to find the formulae for the split consciousness: The true self (existential identity), the false self (contracted self) that is imagined, and the consciousness that must make space for both (comprehensive consciousness). The true self has a genuine identity, the false self has an imagined identity, and comprehensive consciousness has no identity altogether and is, therefore, in constant danger of falling apart (nihilism, if consciousness holds together at all; schizophrenic neurosis, when it does not hold together any longer). Comprehensive consciousness, which has no identity, is the subject of violent revolutionary activism. So far this model of the pneumapathological consciousness has worked well.[4]

Laing's book furnished Voegelin with the formulae he needed to understand these modern intellectuals. He discerned in the works of men such as Hegel, Comte, and Marx what appeared to be two mutually exclusive outlooks on reality. On the one hand, these men were extremely competent critics of their contemporary society and culture, brilliant philosophical physicians who were able precisely to identify and theoretically grasp what was ailing their world. Voegelin identifies this aspect of their work with what he calls in the previous passage their "true self." On the other hand, these same men, in trying to provide solutions to the *accurately diagnosed* problems of their age, tended to exaggerate or overstate their own accomplishments and the extent to which their "systems" achieved truth about reality. They thereby added themselves as additional encumbrances to an already disordered world. Laing's theory of the "two selves" helped Voegelin to understand these contradictory aspects in the psyches of stop-history intellectuals.

The Divided Self is an "existential-phenomenological" account of schizophrenia and schizoid symptoms. In it, Laing did not abide by the traditional approaches of psychiatry, which he believed dehumanize and depersonalize the patient. On the contrary, he presupposes that the patient brings into the treatment situation—whether intentionally or unintentionally and no matter how apparently insane he is—his whole existence—that is, his whole being-in-the-world. Traditional psychiatric practice, which holds that to be "unbiased" one must be as "objective" as possible, treats its patients as dehumanized objects, as creatures whose experience is completely foreign to the experience of "well-adjusted" individuals. For Laing, this "reifying" pseudoscientific approach "must be rigorously resisted."[5] He presumes, furthermore, that every aspect of the patient's being is related in some way to every other aspect, though the manner in which this manifests itself is not always clear. As he states, "It is the task of existential phenomenology to articulate what the other's 'world' is and his way of being in it."[6] The schizoid individual exists "in-the-world" just like every other human being, except in his particular case, something is off, there is a disconnect between himself and this world. The term "schizoid" refers to a person the totality of whose experience is, either through environmental or natural causes, split in two ways. First, there is a division in his relation to the world. Second, there is a division in his relation to himself. This person is unable to experience himself "together with" others or "at home in" the world. Consequently, he experiences himself in despairing aloneness and isolation. What is more, he experiences himself as an incomplete person, as someone who is split in various ways.[7]

In order to clarify the precise nature of this disconnect, Laing contrasts two distinct types of people. There is, on the one hand, the ontologically secure person who—because he experiences himself and others as real, alive, and continuous—is able to confront all of the potential sufferings and dangers of life from a centrally firm sense of his own and other peoples' reality and identity. On the other hand, there is the ontologically insecure person who has a partial or almost complete lack of the assurances that come from an ontologically secure position. Due to the acute anxiety stemming from this insecure position "in-the-world," this person lacks a coherent vision of his own personal identity and normal relationships with others. Laing weighs these two existential positions:

> The individual, then, may experience his own being as real, alive, whole; as differentiated from the rest of the world in ordinary circumstances so clearly that his identity and autonomy are never in question; as a continuum in time; as having an inner consistency, substantiality, genuineness, and worth; as spatially co-extensive with the body; and, usually, as having begun in or around birth and liable to extinction with death. He thus has a firm core of ontological security.

> This, however, may not be the case. The individual in the ordinary circumstances of living may feel more unreal than real; in a literal sense, more dead than alive; he is precariously differentiated from the rest of the world so that his identity and autonomy are always in question. He may lack the experience of his own temporal continuity. He may not possess an overriding sense of personal consistency or cohesiveness. He may feel more insubstantial than substantial, and unable to assume that the stuff he is made of is genuine, good, valuable. And he may feel his self as partially divorced from his body.

> It is, of course, inevitable that an individual whose experience of himself is of this order can no more live in a 'secure' world than he can be secure 'in himself'. The whole 'physiognomy' of his world will be correspondingly different from that of the individual whose sense of self is securely established in its health and validity. Relatedness to other persons will be seen to have a radically different significance and function. To anticipate, we can say that in the individual whose own being is secure in this primary experiential sense, relatedness with others is potentially gratifying; whereas the ontologically insecure person

is preoccupied with preserving rather than gratifying himself: the ordinary circumstances of living threaten his low threshold of security.[8]

To deal with this lack of consistent identity, a person may begin to develop
two or more forms of identity, multiple selves, which help to mediate between
the individual's "true self" and the external world. This "false self" acts as a
barrier protecting the identity of the "true self" from external relations that
might threaten to dissolve, overwhelm, engulf, depersonalize, or implode
it. It functions as a coping mechanism, aiding him in preserving a sense of
identity in what is perceived as a harsh and threatening world.[9] The individual
withdraws into himself—that is, contracts his true self—putting forth a false
exterior while only rarely exposing aspects of his true self.

Rather appropriately, from Voegelin's perspective, Laing brands the series
of affected behaviors, personas, and masks the schizoid individual dons, the
"false-self system." To protect himself from all contingencies and external
situations that might pry open his soul, exposing his true insecure self, the
schizoid individual will develop a very elaborate and sometimes undetect-
able "system" that, because of its predictability, consistently shields him
from threats to his identity. In this way, the individual will have prepared
responses to every situation. He will have multiple false personas that help
him adapt to any unforeseen circumstances. And most importantly, he will
have the *illusion* of being more secure and free than he really is, since his
"false-self system" will shroud reality with a reality of his own making. As
Laing comments,

> Such a schizoid individual in one sense is trying to be *omnipotent* by enclosing
> within his own being, without recourse to a creative relationship with others,
> modes of relationship that require the effective presence to him of other people
> and of the outer world. He would appear to be, in an unreal, impossible way, *all
> persons and things to himself.* The imagined advantages are safety for the true
> self, isolation and hence *freedom from others, self-sufficiency, and control.*[10]

Lurking behind the false-self system are motivations stemming from what
Voegelin, following St. Augustine, will call the *libido dominandi.* Ultimate
power and control, over oneself and others—two things lacking in reality for
human beings—provide the subconscious impetus behind the construction of
the false-self system.

It must be stressed that, for Laing, there is no such thing as a completely
secure person. Every individual, to some degree, manifests schizoid symptoms in his relation to the world, and exhibits some uncertainty about his
personal identity. We all, at some point or another, have put on personas or
developed a "false-self" in order to protect ourselves, in some way, from a

threatening reality. Importantly, one of Laing's essential theses is that *schiz- oid symptoms are not peculiar to full-blown schizophrenics*. Schizophrenia is to be measured by degrees, not by an either/or diagnosis. Some individuals show schizoid characteristics to such a degree that they must be hospitalized. Others can function as "normal" members of society.[11] Because we have a degree of commonality with schizophrenic patients, we are able to sympa- thize and understand them.

NOTES

1. Eric Voegelin, *Selected Correspondence: 1950–1984* (Columbia: University of Missouri Press, 2007), 545.

2. Ibid., 588.

3. See Ibid., where Voegelin acknowledges that modern and ancient Gnostics are indeed very different.

4. Ibid., 555.

5. See R. D. Laing, *The Divided Self: An Existential Study in Sanity and Madness*, location 335 of 3551 in Kindle ebook.

6. Ibid., location 362..

7. Ibid., location 220.

8. Ibid., location 624–637.

9. Ibid., location 651.

10. Ibid., location 1131. My emphasis. It might be interesting to compare this to the passage in the Preface of Hegel's *Phenomenology of Spirit*, where Hegel mentions that he will have to "live" within every shape of spirit.

11. See R. D. Laing, *The Divided Self*, location 195. Also, see Voegelin's enthu- siastic embrace of this approach to psychology in *Selected Correspondence*: 1950– 1984, 546.

Chapter 13

Does Hegel Manifest Schizoid Symptoms?

Turning to the case of Hegel, we see there are a number of factors we must take into account. The most important of these factors is the marked difference between the schizoid symptoms evinced by the normal "average" person and those by a genius of Hegel's stature. Due to his brilliance, Hegel's false-self system will look much different from those studied by R. D. Laing. Indeed, one of Voegelin's major claims is that the grand philosophic systems of the nineteenth century—those of Comte, Hegel, Marx, and Fichte, among others—are essentially the *same sort of device* as those observed in Laing's studies—that is, devices aimed at protecting an individual from a reality he does not accept. According to Voegelin, Hegel manifests these symptoms, but not to such a degree that he would have to be hospitalized. He can function as a relatively well-adjusted member of society and engage in activities perceived as normal. His true self and false self never become completely dissociated.

Voegelin's most thorough and detailed analysis of Hegel's pneumapathological state can be found in "On Hegel: A Study in Sorcery," which begins with a brief analysis of one of Hegel's earliest texts, the *Fortsetzung des "Systems der Sittlichkeit,"* written about 1804–1806 while Hegel was working on the *Phenomenology of Spirit*.[1] In this short incomplete text, Hegel describes his contemporary situation as one of boredom (*Langeweile*) and diremption (*Zerrissenheit*). He goes on to relate that since the "beauty and sacrality" of the pre-Reformation world is lost, and it is impossible to turn back time, history must advance toward a new religious form that understands the first reconciliation of Spirit—that is, the reconciliation inaugurated by Christ—as an "alien sacralization." It must replace it with a sacralization through the Spirit that has become "inward." The new diremption of Spirit that characterizes Hegel's age will be overcome when a "free people" has the audacity, not to receive a religious form, but to *take one* for itself. In

Protestantism, this relation between Spirit and reality has achieved its break-through to consciousness in the medium of philosophy. The philosophy that emerges from Protestant diremption is destined to follow Catholicism and Protestantism as the new, third religion.[2]

But just as Catholicism and Protestantism required real, live historical actors to bring them to fruition—namely, Christ and Luther—so too will this third religion require someone who will inaugurate the new age, articulating its broad outlines and taking the necessary steps to bring it to full actualiza-tion. As Voegelin points out, Hegel's text seems to suggest that Hegel himself is to be this creator of a new age, this founder of a new religion that will overcome the diremption of the time.[3] To appreciate fully the import of this self-designation, one must, in a way, step back from Hegel's rhetoric within his conceptual system to contemplate Hegel the real, live, historical human being. Genius though he was, we must, according to Voegelin, avoid being captured by the self-referential necessity of his logic, so that we never forget its provenance in the psyche of a concrete human being, with his own foibles, insecurities, and shortcomings. It is only by doing this—by contrasting the real concrete Hegel (Hegel in the flesh) with Hegel's self-presentation in his system of thought (Hegel as Messiah), and keeping these divergent images solidly fixed in one's mind—that one can ever truly understand what is prop-erly "modern" in Hegel's existence. As Voegelin states,

> Hence, the modernity of Hegel can be characterized as the coexistence of two selves, as an existence divided into a true and a false self holding one another in such balance that neither the one nor the other ever becomes completely domi-nant. Neither does the true self become strong enough to break the system, nor does the false self become strong enough to transform Hegel into a murderous revolutionary or a psychiatric case.[4]

Just as some of the schizophrenics R. D. Laing analyzes believed them-selves to be all-powerful messiahs or saviors, Hegel greatly exaggerates the degree of certainty his system has achieved and his own importance for the future of humanity. He develops a true, genuine self, which is able to face up to the largest crises of his time. But he also develops a false, inauthentic self, which believes it has achieved certainty about the meaning of existence and the course of history.

Voegelin's diagnosis goes even deeper. For him, these two selves are com-posed of the various strata in Hegel's existence. On one level, according to Voegelin, Hegel really is the great genius he presents himself to be. He truly is a philosopher in the "classic sense" who knew that he could not diagnose the ailments of the age without in some way exempting himself from them. His insight into the various political, religious, cultural, and existential crises of the time are unsurpassed. His existence therefore achieved at least some degree of reconciliation. Otherwise, he could not have recognized the various diremptions of the age for what they were. However, herein lies the limit at which his true and false selves begin to merge. As Voegelin claims, Hegel's very perceptive observations on his age should have awakened in him an acute awareness of his own humanity, along with all of the limitations this humanity implies. But Hegel does not take this final step—a step involving an insight into the truth of his own existence as a man. This step would have really made him effective as a reconciler and restorer of existential order to his contemporaries.[5]

At another level of Hegel's existence is what Voegelin calls the "pneumatism of the inner man and the inner light." Influenced by traditions going back to the sectarian spiritualists of the Middle Ages and Renaissance, as well as Jacob Boehme and the German Pietists, this magical pneumatism resulted in a series of "new Christs" descending upon Europe beginning with the French Revolution.[6] The "savior" aspect in Hegel's consciousness is the first piece of evidence for a constructed false self. Voegelin acknowledges that, insofar as Hegel really did buy into the spirituality of men like Jacob Boehme, he was a very competent spiritualist. However, unfortunately, he also appropriated Boehme's alleged penetration of the Absolute through "picture-thinking" (*Vorstellung*). Hegel goes even further than Boehme in claiming to have given the Christian *Vorstellung* complete conceptual form.[7] His false self thereby awakens and takes its first steps.

The third stratum in his existence is intimately related to the second. It has to do with Hegel's unique egophanic historiogenetic construction of the various historical epochs, which aligns them in such a way that they permit Hegel to imagine the future course of history. By means of this construction, Hegel can "shift the meaning of existence from life in the present under God, with its personal and social duties of the day, to the role of a functionary of history." In this way, "the reality of existence will be eclipsed and replaced by the Second Reality of the imaginative project. . . . [T]he project must first of all eclipse the unknown future by the image of a known future; it must further endow the construction of the ages with the certainty of a science."[8] Leaving aside for now the question of whether or not Hegel's system really does project an imaginative future—something I will argue is *not the case* in the next part of this book—it is clear that this stratum of Hegel's existence is the one at which, for Voegelin, his false self comes fully out into the open.[9] Owing to his "ontological insecurity"—his fear of and unwillingness to accept the harsh mystery of Being—Hegel constructs a system in which both certainty about the meaning of reality and certainty about what is to come in the future are realized.

Hegel's "false-self system" is not a system of behavior made up of various personas and masks—as is the case for schizoids studied by Laing. Rather, it is an outright *conceptual* "system," which allows him to live out a false reality on a theoretical level. This conceptual system serves the same function as the false-self systems of less intellectually inclined schizoids: it protects the insecure true self from what is perceived as a harsh reality that could potentially overwhelm it. It gives the individual a false sense of his own security and omnipotence. Finally, it offers him the illusion of freedom from others who would threaten to undermine his identity. In a passage strikingly similar to Laing's diagnosis of the ultimate reasons behind the construction of a false self, Voegelin states, "The purpose of securing a meaning of existence, with certainty in a masterly role, betrays the motives of the construction in the imaginator's existential insecurity, anxiety, and *libido dominandi*."[10]

NOTES

1. As Voegelin comments in his citation of this text, the MS, now lost, was partly excerpted, partly reported, by Rosenkranz and Haym. A critical edition, based on these reports, was published by Johannes Hoffmeister in *Dokumente zu Hegels Entwicklung* (Stuttgart, 1936), 314–325.

2. Eric Voegelin, "On Hegel: A Study in Sorcery," in *Published Essays: 1966–1985* (Columbia: University of Missouri Press, 1990), 214–215.

3. Hegel did indeed toy with the idea of founding a new religion during his Jena period. He even wrote a brief unpublished pamphlet titled "Religion, Founding a Religion." See Terry Pinkard, *Hegel: A Biography* (New York: Cambridge University Press, 2000), 144.

4. Voegelin, "On Hegel: A Study in Sorcery," 217.

5. Ibid., 215.

6. For a recent analysis of this much forgotten background in Hegel's thought, see Glenn Magee, *Hegel and the Hermetic Tradition* (Ithaca: Cornell University Press, 2001), especially the chapter on the Hermetic influences in the *Phenomenology of Spirit*, 127–149.

7. For a detailed discussion of the relationship between Hegel and Boehme, see Glenn, *Hegel and the Hermetic Tradition*, 138–145.

8. Voegelin, "On Hegel: A Study in Sorcery," 216.

9. I will argue that, once again, it was a reading of Kojève's *Introduction* which influenced Voegelin's own reading. For Kojève, the future of civilization is marked by the gradual spread and increasing power of the "Universal and Homogenous State." Hegel, I will argue in the next chapter, rarely comments on the future course of history; and in the few instances where he does, it is very much in the mode of hypothesis. Voegelin's analysis of the "third stratum" in Hegel's existence—his

supposed certainty about the future—is thus misguided, relying as it does on Kojève's additions.

10. Ibid.

Chapter 14

Shortcomings in Laing's Theory of the Two Selves

Voegelin's appropriation of Laing's theories has its limits. Although he uses Laing's terminology of the two selves for the remainder of his life, Voegelin eventually became critical of the theoretical assumptions implicit in Laing's use of the term "self." His criticism amounted to the insight that Laing's theory spoke of the self in completely immanentist terms. There are no references at all to a transcendent reality in Laing's work, nor to the luminous aspects of consciousness. As Voegelin comments in a later unpublished manuscript, "Laing is keenly sensitive for the 'madness' surrounding us in our society, but he tends, as I have said, to blur the lines that separate a spiritual disorder from a neurosis."[1] His "ontologically insecure" person is considered pathological for no other reason than that he does not accept very basic ontological facts. For instance, he does not accept that he is finite, that he is "one who has had a beginning and who will have an end." He also does not accept that "he has been born and he is going to die" or that "he has a body that roots him to this time and this place."[2] Voegelin's project in the 1970s, including his essay on Hegel, then appears in a new light as an attempt to fit a "two selves" theory within a more comprehensive theory that acknowledges and affirms the experience of transcendence.

Linda C. Raeder formulates this more comprehensive ontology of man:

A "healthy," "balanced," or "well-ordered" consciousness is for Voegelin one that accepts the "tensional structure of existence" and mediates successfully between its contrary poles. "Diseased" or "unbalanced" or "disordered" consciousness, on the other hand, may be defined as a mode of experience wherein one or the other of the existential poles whose tension constitutes the "in-between" reality of human existence has been collapsed; it is existence within a truncated or deformed reality characterized by the eclipse of one or the other of its inseparable dimensions.[3]

The tension of man's existence consists of the divine and human poles playing in tandem at the center of man's consciousness. On the one hand, man is a temporally and spatially located body with biological and physical needs. This "human" pole in man's consciousness is a permanent aspect of his life. No matter how high his spiritual stature, no matter how intellectually competent an individual is, he is ultimately the servant of his body. On the other hand, the "human pole" does not exhaust man's existence. As a participant in Being, as someone whose experience is constituted just as much by It-Reality as Thing-reality—that is, as one who can look back upon history and the entire cosmos and contemplate its ultimate origins and end, and experiences his own life as a part of this larger more comprehensive drama—man's consciousness has what Voegelin calls a "divine pole." This "divine pole" is co-present with the "human pole," and it is the playing out of the tension between these poles that essentially constitutes man's experience of himself in the world.

Unlike Laing, whose understanding of man's consciousness seems hollowed out and one dimensional, Voegelin attempts to do justice to the "multitensional" existence we call human. Laing's theories, while perceptive, do not go beyond a mere description of the transition from a false to a true self. Voegelin, we might say, attempts to root this "ontological insecurity" in the inability to mediate successfully between the human and divine poles of man's consciousness. Out of the depths of this insecurity, individuals can imaginatively "eclipse" one of these essential poles. One can eclipse the transcendent divine pole, in which case the individual absorbs the divinity into himself, resulting in the self-perception that one is a God or "thinks the thoughts of God before creation."[4] Or one can eclipse the human pole of existence, resulting in an individual who views himself as disembodied or completely separate from all material existence.[5]

Voegelin calls attention to the Greek symbol "Nous" as an adequate expression of the ordering force in man's psyche that helps mediate these layers of his existence. Man is not a disembodied psyche, just as he is equally not pure "material." Man's "integral nature"—as Voegelin calls it—comprises both the *noetic psyche*—that part of man's consciousness seeking divine order—and man's participation in the hierarchy of being, reaching down from man's psyche to the physical, chemical, and biological layers underlying it.[6] The authentically human form of existence, therefore, is one of *tension toward* the divine ground of his existence. It is a *questioning unrest* for the ultimate wherefrom and whereto of his existence, for its ground and meaning.

Human beings can either remain open to the mystery of the ultimate wherefrom and whereto of existence—a mystery that extends beyond the individual's own life—or attempt to gain a counterfeit closure by constructing a false self and the false-self system resulting from it. Laing roots this attempt to gain closure in the individual's unwillingness to accept the undeniable conditions of life. However, he does not thoroughly elucidate what these conditions are. Voegelin is unreservedly in line with him up to this point, but makes an effort to fully articulate these ever-present realities, the most important of which is the reality of transcendence—the reality of the human *incapacity* to ever pronounce definitively on the meaning of his existence.

NOTES

1. Eric Voegelin, "The Eclipse of Reality," in *What Is History? and Other Late Unpublished Writings*, eds. Thomas Hollweck and Paul Caringella (Columbia: University of Missouri Press, 1990), 161.

2. R. D. Laing, *The Divided Self: An Existential Study in Sanity and Madness*, location 362 of 3551 in Kindle ebook.

3. Linda C. Raeder, "Voegelin on Gnosticism, Modernity, and the Balance of Consciousness," in *VoegelinView*, 345.

4. Georg W. F. Hegel, *The Science of Logic*, tr. A. V. Miller (Amherst: Humanity Books, 1969), 50. One should at least mention here some of the more obvious ways individuals have "eclipsed the divine pole" of their existence. Specifically, Voegelin points to atheism, materialism, and secularism as the most common forms. Hegel's eclipsing of the divine pole is unique in this respect insofar as he attempts to absorb the divine into himself.

5. On the disembodied self, see R. D. Laing, *The Divided Self*, location 971 of 3551.

6. "Reason: The Classic Experience," 268.

Chapter 15

Ontological Insecurity and Von Doderer's Analysis of Second Realities

As can be grasped from the preceding analysis, Voegelin was not shy about using other authors' fully worked-out theories for his own purposes.[1] Voegelin's own originality comes not from developing his own method or theoretical principles, but from his willingness to appropriate insights already achieved and apply them to areas of reality that have not yet been theoretically explored. Another theorist to whom Voegelin is indebted in this respect is the novelist Heimito Von Doderer, whose masterpiece, *The Demons*, is an unsurpassed exploration of the human psyche living in an ideological climate.[2] Along with the principles discovered in Laing's theory of the divided self, Von Doderer's analysis of "Second Realities" provided the theoretical background for Voegelin's efforts to understand the peculiar brand of ideology characteristic of end of history speculators. Out of the depths of ontological insecurity, the split-self will necessarily construct an imaginative Second Reality, which will cause innumerable areas of friction with First Reality, the only true reality. In what follows, I will give a brief overview of some of the main speculative threads woven throughout *The Demons* so as to clarify Voegelin's own views on Second Realities.

The plot of the novel centers around the political events leading up to the burning of the Palace of Justice in Vienna on July 15, 1927—an event that is not to be understood apart from the theoretical core of the book. However, one could argue that the *speculative* pivot-point of *The Demons* occurs at an otherwise insignificant table-tennis party taking place in the apartment of one of the novel's main characters, Grete Siebenschein. In the course of a casual conversation between René Stangeler, a gifted intellectual and expert on Merovingian Medieval history, and Jan Herzka, the owner of a webbing factory with a peculiar interest in witch trials, the interlocutors broach the topic of the subtle difference between "hallucinations" and the imaginative fabric of consciousness. When Angelika Trapp, a person of rather limited intelligence, writes off the religious experiences of those living in the Middle Ages as mere "hallucinations," Stangeler offers to explain why it is impossible to apply a contemporary vocabulary to the basic experiential phenomena of the Middle Ages. By the word "hallucination," one usually implies a more or less neurotic or hysterical mental state. But, he claims, it would be a misunderstanding to apply this same word to a time in which these supposed "hallucinations" made up the basic fabric of every *healthy* consciousness. Stangeler explains: "History is not at all knowledge of the past, but in actuality the science of the future—of, that is, whatever in the given segment we are studying was to be the future, or *hoped to be*. There we find what really happened. . . . [T]hen you understand that its task (history's) is to find the corresponding spring-house, the corresponding frog of the bow, for everything that afterwards acquired a name."[3] In the Middle Ages, the hoped-for future (the "hereafter in the here") consisted of a vast wealth of imaginative symbols, including devils, demons, monsters, and angels. In the twentieth century, human beings continue to hope for some unrealizable "hereafter in the here." However, because the modern consciousness is less and less permeated by the imaginative symbols that would allow us to maintain a healthy equilibrium in our psyche, our hoped-for future ends up taking the form of idiosyncratic sexual obsessions and/or political ideologies. Our age, according to Stangeler, has almost entirely lost that healthy power of imagination with which individuals found their bearings in earlier epochs of history. Because of this loss, we tend to classify that imaginative power as a sickness, though in reality it is not. "Rather," Stangeler continues,

> it has its place within the picture of the whole man just as much as other powers of the body and psyche. We, however, are familiar with such phenomena only in madmen; in our times the mysterious course of disease can split the psyche of some poor chap so wide that we see down to the traditional, inherited materials which lie at the bottom, under deep layers of slag. But when, nowadays, this inheritance wells up, it can only form strange bubbles that soon burst. In a state of vigorous health—and that is the only valid criterion—no one possesses that imaginative capacity any longer. In our civilization, its very appearance deforms the personality, makes its possessor a kind of freak. Or else it is found in conjunction with schizoid mental disease. In our times, a person who could command such an imagination while remaining in healthy balance would be a monster. But in those days such a person was entirely normal.[4]

These lines require some elucidation. First, it should be stressed that throughout the novel, the theme of the "hereafter in the here"—the hoped-for future making up the "spring-house" of the present—recurs in a variety of different existential contexts. What Stangeler voices as the hermeneutical key to under-standing history applies just as well to an analysis of the novel as a whole. Von Doderer's purpose is to understand the ideological makeup of Vienna just prior to the establishment of an Authoritarian government and the subsequent *Anschluss* into the Nazi Third Reich. One could say that Von Doderer is, throughout his novel, formulating the same sort of historical study Stangeler outlines. He is looking back upon the Vienna of the 1920s from the perspec-tive of a post–World War II Europe with the hopes of discovering the "frog of the bow" that eventuated in Austria's collapse. He is attempting to unearth the seeds of the various political ideologies in Europe, and analyze the existential weakness that allowed these ideologies to predominate. The "hereafter in the here"—the various views on the way reality ought to be rather than the way reality is—is, it seems, one of the major driving forces in the construction of these political ideologies, left and right. Second, it is, I argue, one of the principal theses of Von Doderer's novel that this lack of imaginative capacity on the part of modern man is precisely the major distorting element in his existence. Because modern man is not attuned in a healthy way to the forces in the psyche that require this imagination for their full and accurate expres-sion, he is more likely to compensate by constructing an obsessive "Second Reality." As Stangeler comments, when this occurs, it is likely that it will well up, forming strange bubbles that soon burst as they come into contact with First Reality.

As the narrative of *The Demons* unfolds, Von Doderer introduces several other characters with their own unique Second Reality projections—their own "hereafters in the here." As a result of being so preoccupied with the hoped-for image of their Second Reality (their "hereafter"), these characters fall victim to a distorted view of their present situation (their "here"). This distortion affects their relationships with friends, their careers, or their views on the possibilities and limitations of politics. To use a frequently recurring image in the novel, these men are like fetuses in the womb covering their eyes with their hands lest their peaceful tranquility be disturbed by too much light.[5] The desire for order in their own personal lives and in the political realm, while in itself a praiseworthy goal, becomes an *obsession* the Second Reality is supposed to aid in bringing to fruition. Hoping to construct a "Tower of Babel to the God of Order out of the building materials of life, which as always lie around in jumbled heaps," these individuals, in the end, do nothing more than create "an extremely high hat which they must balance so care-fully on their heads that they don't dare take a step forward." In the words of the novel's narrator, Georg von Gyrenhoff, "The smallest nothing upsets the 'growing oneness and tranquility' of such a life. This oneness is nothing but the rigid pattern, the establishment of a second life, an antilife."[6]

The range of these second realities is extensive, but in Von Doderer's presentation, they usually take the form of obsessive sexual fantasies or political ideologies. Kajetan von Schlaggenberg, a moderately successful novelist and dandy, finds himself dealing with a temporary obsession with "fat ladies," while Jan Herzka, a wealthy factory owner who inherits a castle, has a sado-masochistic fixation on his secretary Agnes Gebeaur. He imagines her as an accused witch in the Middle Ages, undergoing torture aimed at forcing a confession. These men are, on an existential level, no different from the various political ideologues one sees throughout the novel as well. Imre von Gyurkicz is a self-important newspaper cartoonist and Social Democrat who lives in a sea of his own lies about himself and his past. His entire life consists of a variety of "emblems"—for example, his revolver or a skull in his apartment—about whose origins he tells lies to maintain a persona in front of his friends and acquaintances. What is characteristic of Gyurkicz's Second Reality is that the fabricated and illusory past he has created for himself does not function as a mask in which he himself does not believe. Instead, he himself *actually believes his own lies*—that is, he fully lives and breathes the fantastical creation of his own life.

Gyurkicz is, in many ways, Von Doderer's quintessential political ideologue, whose Second Reality leads to his becoming a martyred revolutionary during the riots that led to the burning of the Palace of Justice. This typical political ideologue, or revolutionary, lives in a world of generalizations, since he has departed from "the tangible and concrete." He wants to change the "fundaments of life in general" because he has been unable to endure himself. The highly concrete task of his own life, with which he has been unable to cope, has to be consigned to oblivion. When this happens, the slogan is born. Immediacy, concreteness, and direct relationships to friendly persons are buried. Henceforth, all such relationships depend less upon emotional affinities and more on the "intricacies of a doctrine" that has been installed "more or less as a regulator of relationships among human beings."[7] One might, for instance, associate with individuals one finds morally reprehensible or with whom one is in no way compatible for the simple reason that one shares their particular ideological convictions. Likewise, one may hate or refuse to associate with individuals with whom one would naturally be friends, such as close family members. All of this stems, according to Von Doderer's Stangeler, from the incapacity to perceive reality and the cold hard facts of which it is composed.

The creation of a Second Reality, and the tension between it and First Reality, is a peculiarly modern phenomenon, having to do with the loss of imaginative symbolisms that helped order consciousness in the past. In the Middle Ages, such a Second Reality would have been called a Demon. Yet, in the twentieth century, Stangeler remarks, "such a thing is falsely called a philosophy." He continues, "But the mutual hatred that constantly breaks out between these rival philosophies should tell us something. That alone should indicate that their real source has nothing to do with divergent opinions on how 'humanity' can be helped, or in this class or that race . . . and suchlike idiocies."[8] All fixations, whether sexual, political, or ethical, distort one's view of a highly diverse and manifold present. These are our modern "Demons."

It seems that the only alternative to constructing one of these Second Realities is, for Von Doderer, not only to accept the plain and apparent conditions of life, with all of their hardships and complications, but also to strive to live with *prudence*, the virtue equivalent to the ability to apperceive reality as it is rather than as it ought to be. It is only when one is first able to see reality clearly, in all of its dimensions, that one can then act sensibly for one's own good and the good of others. As Von Gyrenhoff reflects on Stangeler's radical transformation of character from someone blinded and hindered by a Second Reality to a man learning to live with prudence,

> For he himself was there, altogether himself, and circumspect, and quick-thinking, examining things in perspective, prudently checking all possibilities. Prudently—for prudence came easy to him now, had become natural and proper. "That is the true order which supports a person, the real order, not some chancy fabricated one. These fellows all want to live in a prolongation of their own imagination. Just like Herzka. Otherwise they hold their hands over their eyes. An embryo in the womb."[9]

When one becomes obsessed with an image of the way reality should be, one loses the ability to properly assess reality as it is.[10] What arises then is a neurotic obsession with trying to eliminate those aspects of reality that do not conform to one's image of it—or, at least, with constructing one's life in such a way that one does not have to "apperceive" these recalcitrant and inconvenient aspects of reality.

NOTES

1. See Voegelin's rather arresting comment that "the test of truth, to put it pointedly, will be the lack of originality in the propositions" ("Equivalences of Experience and Symbolization in History," *Published Essays: 1966–1985* [Columbia: University of Missouri Press, 1990]), 122.

2. See Voegelin's 1957 letter to Robert Heilman, in which he mentions Von Doderer's influence on his understanding of "Second Realities" and their role in the creation of an ideological environment, in *Selected Correspondence: 1950–1984* (Columbia: University of Missouri Press, 2007), 306.

3. Heimito von Doderer, *The Demons* (Alfred A. Knopf, 1961), 452–453. My emphasis.

4. Ibid., 453–454.

5. Ibid., 494.

6. Ibid., 375.

7. Ibid., 491.

8. Ibid., 1018.

9. Ibid., 750.

10. Compare Voegelin's other criterion of truth, which is that it must stand up against the following question: "Do we have to ignore and eclipse a major part of the historical field in order to maintain the truth of the propositions?" ("Equivalences of Experience and Symbolization," 122).

Chapter 16

Voegelin on Hegel's Second Reality

Von Doderer's analysis of the "refusal to apperceive" becomes a crucial part of Voegelin's own efforts to critique twentieth-century ideology. Voegelin maintains that this refusal is the peculiar enigma of modernity.[1] It results in what he eventually calls the "Eclipse of Reality," which occurs when a person is so ideologically fixated on an idea that all other unchangeable aspects of reality are forgotten about or ignored altogether. After a lifetime of studying sound thinkers—most notably, Plato, Aristotle, and their philosophic and mythological predecessors—along with both Von Doderer's vocabulary of First and Second Realities and R. D. Laing's terminology of the two selves, Voegelin has the conceptual apparatus necessary to dissect the various types of deformed existence he sees in the stop-history movements. That part of an individual's existential core that recognizes and is attuned to First Reality Voegelin terms their True Self. That part that projects an imaginative Second Reality or a False Self-System is the False Self or, alternatively, the Contracted Self.

As previously mentioned, Voegelin is convinced that the peculiar ailment of modern thinkers is a contraction of the individual's humanity to a self imprisoned in its own selfhood. Since the man who engages in this self-deformation never ceases to be a man, and the surrounding fourfold reality of God and man, world and society does not change its structure, areas of friction between the shrunken self and reality are bound to develop. Moreover, as the man who contracts his humanity will be disinclined to leave the prison of his selfhood to remove these frictions, he would much rather, according to Voegelin, put his "imagination to further good use by surrounding the imaginary self with an imaginary reality constructed to confirm the self in its counterfeit reality. He will create a Second Reality in order to screen the First Reality of Common experience from his view."[2] Thus, reality will no longer be apperceived or expressed as it is, but will appear or be expressed in terms of the individual's resistance to it.

Voegelin formulated four rules governing the dynamics of the creation and perpetuation of Second Realities. These are as follows:

1. When imaginators of Second Realities proceed to act on their imaginative assumptions and try to make the world of common experience conform to their respective dreams, the areas of friction with reality will rapidly increase in number and size.
2. As the world of common experience can be eclipsed but not abolished, it will resist its deformation and, in its turn, force the imaginators to revise their Second Realities. Imaginative projecting will not be given up as senseless, but specific projects will be changed in detail or replaced by new ones.
3. When conflicts with reality compel revisions with some frequency over a period, the activity of projecting can pass from a phase of comparatively naïve indulgence to one of a more critical occupation with the standards of projects. For a Second Reality must, on the one hand, satisfy the requirements of the contracted self and, on the other hand, contain enough uneclipsed reality not to be ignored as a crackpot scheme by the contemporaries. There is a remarkable advance from the comparatively loose anthropologies and philosophies of history of the eighteenth century to the tight interlocking of Hegel's *Phaenomenologie, Logik, Philosophie des Rechts,* and *Philosophie der Geschichte.*
4. When a more or less stable balance between the contracted self and the satisfactory Second Realities has been achieved—as it has in the work of Comte, Hegel, and Marx—the interest can shift from the construction of further Second Realities to the problems of deformation.[3]

A cursory glance at these rules reveals that Voegelin believed Hegel to be both the *inheritor* of Second Realities already formulated in the eighteenth century and the creator of his own. Hegel's system represents, among other things, a very refined, detailed, and precise articulation of the premises involved in prior Secondary Realities. It is a continuation of the Eclipse of Reality begun in the Enlightenment. Furthermore, we see here that Hegel's Second Reality is, viewed from Voegelin's perspective, nothing more than an *intermediary stage* in the historical cycle of Secondary Realities, the beginning of which is characterized by the naively optimistic hubris of the Enlightenment, and the end of which is characterized by the dark despair of nihilism. Hegel, for this reason, deserves to be Voegelin's primary target, since he, more than anybody else, demonstrates in an unabashed way the peculiar intellectual mechanisms involved in constructing and promoting a

Second Reality. While many others before him have expressed similar premises and intentions, Hegel is perhaps the most explicit and forthright about his maneuvers.

But what are these intellectual maneuvers that, according to Voegelin, succeed in obscuring the true human condition? Voegelin highlights three specific maneuvers all end of history speculators engage in, but that Hegel most clearly expressed. The first has to do with Hegel's invention of an entirely new speculative language to construct his system.[4] This speculative language employs very common German words, whose meanings are subsequently altered or rendered ambiguous when fit into the system. Though Voegelin would acknowledge this is common practice among many thinkers, Hegel's linguistic creations appear to serve a very specific function. They allow the undoubted ambiguity of his pronouncements to conceal what it is he is really doing.[5]

The meaning of the terms *Geist* (Spirit), *Gedanke* (Thought), *Begriff* (Concept), *Vorstellung* (Conception), and *Idee* (Idea) seem to shift or carry several different meanings throughout Hegel's analyses. As one particular example, Voegelin points to the terms *Geist* and *Gedanke* as possible synonymous translations of the Greek word *Nous*. However, if one assumes this identification, then Hegel's statement that Thought has come to govern the Spiritual world would no longer make sense. If we assume that these terms are not synonymous, and that only Thought translates *Nous*, then what is meant by the "Spirit it has come to govern"? But then if we look at other statements Hegel makes—for instance, that the world has been pervaded by the enthusiasm of the Spirit, now that Thought has come to govern the world—it sounds as if "Thought and Spirit were actually the same."[6] These terms only make sense, according to Voegelin, if one enters into the self-referential necessity of Hegel's Second Reality. If this occurs, it becomes clear that the

> Nous of Anaxagoras and Aristotle will be the divine Spirit that governs a world removed from divinity; Thought will be the name of the divine Spirit when, in the dialectical course of history, it has gained the "objective form" of human thinking that enables it "to reach effectively into external reality" because now it is immanent to the world in which it operates; and the Spiritual World will be the world of man, society, and history in which the divine Spirit, having gained the objective form of human thought, operates effectively.[7]

The purpose of Hegel's ambiguous use of these terms becomes clear. Their meaning only makes sense in the context of Hegel's system, along with all of the theoretical premises contained in it. Hegel's vocabulary has a self-referential necessity that, from the perspective of an outside observer living in First Reality, appears to be nonsensical, but which has a certain convincing power from the perspective of Hegel's Second Reality.

The second major mechanism Hegel uses to eclipse reality is a direct consequence of the first. He argues for the truth of his "scientific system" in a language that derives its own validity as a conceptual language from the science whose truth it wants to establish. In other words, the system proves itself to be the one and only truth of reality by the sheer fact of its being constructed.[8] Unlike some of the other mechanisms Hegel uses to eclipse reality, we can discover this one rather easily on the surface of his work. One can find an explicit statement to this effect in the introduction to *The Science of Logic*.[9] Hegel's system is justifiably deemed "circular," since it presupposes what it sets out to prove—namely, that Absolute Knowledge has been achieved in the system, and that this system can only prove its validity in the act of being constructed.

The third mechanism deals with Hegel's interpretation of the entire history of philosophy as a preparation for himself. This mechanism has already been treated in detail in our chapter on "Gnostic Historiogenesis." As Voegelin notes, "The imaginator Hegel protects the *perpetuum mobile* of his self-contained and self-moving System of Science against confrontation with reality by interpreting the representatives of existential truth as the forerunners of the truth that has come to the clarity of consciousness in his system."[10] He performs this mechanism by deliberately distorting the truth these forerunners represent. In the case of Plato, for instance, Hegel views the dialogues as attempts to achieve the same conceptual clarity about reality that Hegel does in his own system. When these dialogues fall short of their goal—specifically, in their employment of myth—it is because Plato found himself living in an historical epoch when the truth about reality would have been impossible to grasp. Though the myths are charming and pedagogically useful, from Hegel's standpoint, they "betray Plato's inability to penetrate certain areas of the *Geist* by *Gedanke*."[11] For Hegel, images distort thought. Since they appeal to our imagination, they will never break free into the dry, crisp air of thought.

Hegel's comments on Plato's relationship to the truth contained in his own system strike Voegelin as a deliberate falsification. In Voegelin's eyes, Plato's use of myth manifests, not his failure as a thinker, but his critical understanding of philosophical analysis and its limitations. To quote Voegelin at length,

> The philosopher can clarify the structure and process of consciousness, he can draw more clearly the line between the reality of consciousness and the reality of which it is conscious; but he can neither expand man's consciousness into the reality in which it is an event, nor contract reality into the event of consciousness. Plato knows quite well that his myth—of Eros, of the psyche as the

site of man's search for the divine ground of his existence, of the immortality of the soul, of its pre- and post-existence, its guilt and purification, of the last judgment, of the demiurgic origin of the cosmos—symbolizes experiences of the *Geist*, but he also knows that man's *Geist* is not identical with the reality in which it participates consciously through experience. The experience of participation in a divinely ordered Cosmos extending beyond man can be expressed only by means of the myth; it cannot be transformed into processes of thought within consciousness.[12]

In other words, Plato was acutely aware of man's *consubstantiality* with divine reality, but never went so far as to extend this consubstantiality into an "identity-in-difference." Only Hegel is guilty of this error. The proper medium to express this consubstantiality is myth, as it preserves the realities of both our nearness to and distance from the divine ground. For Voegelin, Plato is unsurpassed in this regard. He is not a philosophical forerunner to better philosophies to come in the future. If there ever was a philosopher who fully grasped the human condition in all its dimensions, it was Plato. Hegel, in order to interpret him as a forerunner to his system, has to distort Plato's work to fit it into the schema of his Second Reality.

These three aspects in Hegel's work—his invention of an ambiguous new language, the circular logic used to prove the validity of the system, and his interpretation of all previous philosophers as forerunners to himself—derive from that part of Hegel's existence Voegelin calls his False Self, and consequently are used as devices for masking his imaginative Second Reality. They are not merely the result of honest theoretical mistakes. They can be regarded as the direct result of Hegel's existential deficiencies. According to Voegelin, Hegel suffered from "ontological insecurity." Due to his existential weakness, he simply could not accept basic ontological facts about the human condition—such as, transcendence, uncertainty about the future, authentic interpersonal relationships, or the luminous dimension of consciousness. In Voegelin's eyes, Hegel was an absolutely monumental figure, an intellect of vast proportions, whose insights span the entire spectrum of human existence. But this great mind was, at the end of the day, unable to cope with his humanity and, consequently, was transformed into a monstrosity. We are still dealing with the tragic consequences of his thought today.

NOTES

1. See Voegelin's 1977 letter to Michael Platt, in *Selected Correspondence: 1950–1984* (Columbia: University of Missouri, 2007), 820.

2. Eric Voegelin, "The Eclipse of Reality," in *What Is History? And Other Late Unpublished Writings*, eds. Thomas Hollweck and Paul Caringella (Columbia: University of Missouri Press, 1990), 111–112.

3. Ibid., 118.

4. Ibid.

5. See "On Hegel: A Study in Sorcery," 228, where Voegelin claims, "It makes almost no sense to ask what Hegel really meant. The interpreter must be alert to the games of the divided Self. He must put Hegel into quotation marks, because no statement concerning 'Hegel's' intentions can be valid, unless it takes into account the intricate movements of his Selfs."

6. Voegelin, "The Eclipse of Reality," 118.

7. Ibid., 119.

8. Ibid., 149.

9. See Hegel's *Science of Logic*, tr. A.V. Miller (Amherst: Humanity Books, 1969), 43.

10. Voegelin, "The Eclipse of Reality," 150.

11. Eric Voegelin, "On Hegel: A Study in Sorcery," in *Published Essays: 1966–1985* (Columbia: University of Missouri Press, 1990), 232. In this same passage, Voegelin quotes Hegel's *Vorlesungen über die Geschichte der Philosophie*, Vol. II (Jubilaumsausgabe, ed. Glockner), 188–189.

12. Ibid., 233.

Chapter 17

Voegelin's Kojèvian "Code" as an Inadequate Interpretation of Hegel's System

Voegelin's interpretation of Hegel's system as an imaginative Second Reality that "eclipses" First Reality depends upon a peculiar understanding of Hegel and his theoretical presuppositions. Voegelin focuses, for example, on the "third stratum" in Hegel's existence as the one that constitutes his false self. This is the stratum that reveals Hegel's projecting of an imaginative future and his messianic ambitions to inaugurate it. Much of the rest of his critique simply assumes that this "third stratum" is an integral part of Hegel's thought. For Voegelin, Hegel's existential deficiencies depend upon his unwillingness to accept the ultimate mystery of the future, of transcendence, of political and historical reality. And, therefore, his supposed messianism is a device to obscure and eclipse these mysteries.

However, there are some defects in Voegelin's assumptions about Hegel. As will be shown in the following chapter, scholars do not agree that this messianic stratum exists in Hegel's thought. In fact, many interpreters of Hegel's work argue for a much less certain, much less definitive system. What I will argue in the next section is that Kojève, on certain fundamental points, *misunderstood* Hegel. He got Hegel wrong. Unlike the portrait of a man sitting on his throne at the end of history, capable of answering every question about every aspect of reality, the Hegel whose picture I will paint is not quite as sure of himself or the future course of historical events. Indeed, his future is extremely blurry, *if not impossible* to know. It is only in Kojève's *Introduction* that we get this idyllic image of the future state of society, in the Universal and Homogeneous State. It is Kojève, not Hegel, who pronounces definitively upon the future state of society and thereby attempts to gain existential closure. Hegel, perhaps in a more radical way than any of his predecessors, *refused* to claim any knowledge about the future course of history. The future, for him, remained an incomprehensible mystery. In fact, an integral part of his thought is the systematic exposition of why this inability to pronounce on the future is a necessary part of the human condition.

This is not to say we should consider everything in Voegelin's critique irrelevant. Insofar as it has to do with the genuine assumptions with which Hegel was working, it can be viewed as one of the most penetrating and insightful critiques in the twentieth century. I believe Voegelin is certainly not wrong in detecting traces of hubris and naïve optimism in Hegel's consciousness. It is undeniable, especially when one looks at the work of his younger years, that Hegel regarded his work as an unsurpassable synthesis of all that came before him and as a threshold into a new world and new age. It is also impossible to refute the fact that he may have allocated to himself an inordinate amount of importance in his interpretation of history. But these aspects of his work and biography must be seen in their true light. We cannot extrapolate from them to the conclusion that Hegel believed himself to be a messiah.

The following chapter argues neither that Voegelin's critique depends *entirely* upon Kojève's skewed interpretation of Hegel's system, nor that Kojève got Hegel completely wrong. Rather, I will simply suggest that alternative interpretations of Hegel's system exist that might succeed in more adequately defending Hegel against his Voegelinian detractors. One is not obliged to regard Kojève's *Introduction* as definitive, as Voegelin did. Though it is replete with remarkable insights into Hegel's *Phenomenology of Spirit*, it should not be seen as the authoritative "code" we must use to crack the system, since it neither does justice to some of the later developments in Hegel's thought, nor meets Hegel's system head on, but simply assumes very basic Marxist presuppositions, which are foreign to Hegel's thought. In what follows, I will rely rather heavily upon the work of two relatively recent Hegelians—namely, Slavoj Zizek and Eric Michael Dale—who have made a considerable amount of headway in dispelling some of the myths surrounding Hegel's thought. Both authors reconceive Hegel in a refreshingly radical new light. Our fifth part will take a look at Hegel's understanding of the future in an effort to discern precisely how, in his mind, *history would continue* in completely new, unforeseeable ways. In doing this, we will critique, *from a Hegelian perspective*, Kojève's outlook on the Universal and Homogeneous State. In addition, this final section will examine the meaning of Hegelian Absolute Knowing. In so doing, we will discover that, contrary to Kojève's assertions, Absolute Knowledge does *not* mean the ability to answer every question about every aspect of reality. It is simply the systematic exposition of the full set of conditions for rationality and knowing anything at all. There is still room for transcendence in Hegel's system.

PART V

Kojève's Hegel: Deliberate Falsification or Valid Exegesis?

Chapter 18

Possible Interpretations of End of History Thesis

The goal of this section is twofold. As we have now come to a point in our analysis where we can shift our focus from Voegelin's critique of the End of History thesis to an explication of what Hegel in fact said about the End of History, it would first of all be appropriate to clarify all of its possible variants. One of the shortcomings in Voegelin's critique of Hegel is that he, using the general phrase "stop-history movements," tends to obfuscate the very pronounced differences between what Hegel means by the End of History and what other authors, like Marx and Kojève, suggest by the idea. If one is to come to an adequate understanding of the contemporary globalized political and economic landscape, it is crucial to make these key distinctions.

Separating Kojève's interpretation of Hegel from Hegel's actual theories is the second aspect of this section's twofold goal. Once we have organized all of the possible variants of the End of History thesis, a greater explanation of the complexities of Kojève's and Hegel's positions will be warranted. This final part will thus consist of an argument for the uniqueness of Hegel's stance on the End of History. I will not necessarily argue that Hegel repudiates the End of History idea. I will suggest instead that his version of it is more philosophically tenable than Kojève's caricature.

Let us begin with a preliminary outline of the possible interpretations of the End of History thesis. Some of these will be explained in greater detail in the next chapter.

1. The End of History is a static, globalized, universal, and homogeneous political and economic order characterized by unending technological progress. In this world, the Last Man takes the stage. There are possible Communist, Capitalist, and synthetic brands of this thesis. Marx, Kojève, and Francis Fukuyama argue for this variant of the End of History.

2. The End of History means the *teleological completion* of history. In this understanding, history has come to its end, but this does not necessitate that the status quo will be preserved indefinitely. Rather, like an organism that has achieved its teleological completion, the global political and economic order will begin to decay, for whatever reason. This, I will argue, is one viable interpretation of Hegel's work.

3. The End of History is a misleading ideological stance that only conceals power struggle. This End of History is inextricably linked to Western hegemony. It is built on power, not reason and persuasion. This state of contemporary culture and politics only displays the self-delusions of Westerners. Zizek and many Postmodern philosophers critique from this position, while geopolitical Realists, like John Mearsheimer and Henry Kissinger, advocate it.

4. The End of History means the completion or end of an *historical era*, but not necessarily of "history" strictly speaking. The future, after one historical era is over, contains possibilities that are impossible to see from our present historical standpoint. The only thing we can be sure about is that "reason" will manifest itself somehow. Following Michael Dale and Zizek, I will argue that this is another viable interpretation of Hegel's system.

5. The End of History presupposes a false philosophical anthropology that misunderstands what is fundamentally satisfying for human beings. Samuel Huntington, in his book *The Clash of Civilizations and the Remaking of World Order*, argues for this thesis. This version is also part of Voegelin's critical stance.

6. As revealed in the Book of Revelation, the End of History is the Christian Apocalyptic End of History. A secularized version of this thesis, combined with the Aristotelian concept of *telos*, is responsible for the exaggerations of (1).

7. The End of History will be the self-induced destruction of mankind from nuclear war, environmental catastrophe, meteor, or the like.

For the purposes of this section, the relevant possibilities are (1), (2), (3), (4), and (5), as they are within the range of human control and bear on our discussion of Kojève's misreading of Hegel. Though (6) and (7) might very well be accurate in their description of how history will end, they are completely outside the range of Hegel's discourse and thus do not bear on our discussion of Hegel's End of History thesis.

What is essentially at stake in all of these variants is the meaning, significance, and existence of *teleology* in history. Every form of the End of History thesis presupposes that history has a *telos*, though what this *telos* signifies varies. History, if it is to have an end, must have a beginning and an essence that can be *completed or finished*. When Aristotle speaks of teleology, he addresses the complexity in the life-cycles of living creatures, which show a large variation in their potentialities as they develop to maturity and eventually die.[1] One thing that is interesting, however, is that he never entertains the notion that teleological completion might be equated with immortality. Some End of History speculators do suggest this equation in regard to political orders. For Aristotle, a creature's actualizing its *telos* immediately precedes its gradual decay and death. So, it is not out of bounds to ask how it could even be implied that the teleological completion of history meant a political, economic, and cultural *status quo* that would remain indefinitely. Marx, Fukuyama, and Kojève argue this precise thing in variant (1). An idea unrelated to the notion of an Aristotelian *telos* must have been introduced into their cultural milieu for this to be possible. Could this be an effect of the influence of Christianity, loosely interpreted, on the question of history?

In light of this question, I might suggest that perhaps Hegel has been so horribly misunderstood because interpreters have viewed his vague statements about the End of History as secularized Christian Apocalypticism rather than as exclusively Aristotelian. The problem with the former view is that it has very little basis in what Hegel actually says. The latter standpoint, on the other hand, is substantiated at all levels of Hegel's thought, from his *Logic* to his *Philosophy of Right*. The main thesis of this section is that Kojève (deliberately?) misunderstands Hegel on precisely this point. From what his texts actually suggest, Hegel maintains either standpoint (2) or (4). Voegelin's criticisms of Hegel's apparent historical and philosophical closure, while perhaps valid up to a certain point, are misguided in their reliance on Kojève's *Introduction* as an interpretive "code."

NOTES

1. In regard to our specific topic, Aristotle claims that the Polis undergoes a natural development, as it waxes and wanes and the arts/sciences decline and then are recovered again and again for eternity. Philosophy will pass back into mythology and mythology will rise once again to philosophy. Given the notion of teleological completion in the human community, it seems that Hegel holds a view similar to Aristotle's notion of development and decline in an eternal universe. For a full-length study on Hegel's close relationship to Aristotle, see Alfredo Ferrarin, *Hegel and Aristotle* (New York: Cambridge University Press).

Chapter 19

Kojève on the Present and Future

This chapter will examine viewpoints (1) and (3) since the two are linked.[1] As Shadia B. Drury argues, viewpoint (3) is simply a critique of viewpoint (1). The leftist and rightist postmodern reaction—exemplified in the works of Foucault, Bataille, Strauss, Bloom, Zizek, and Derrida—to the rigid and lifeless rationalism of modernity has its origins in Kojève's influence on the French intellectual scene in the mid-twentieth century. The modernity to which these men react was simply the caricature of modernity presented in Kojève's reading of Hegel. Drury makes the case that the original sin of our contemporary political predicament was a misunderstanding of Hegel. This misunderstanding shapes both left-wing and right-wing political rhetoric in contemporary America.[2]

To begin, what did Kojève actually say about the future course of history? The Alexandre Kojève known to most academics is famous for stating that the End of History will see the Universal and Homogeneous State take over the globe. He was a man whose entire life was dedicated to this thesis, as he worked to spread it both theoretically (through his lecture courses) and concretely (through his work in the French Ministry of Finance). He held the view that as Nation-States die out due to globalization, native ethnic cultures will fade away and human beings will gradually become more identical in their thoughts, habits, and activities. Economic activity will have a universal, global significance, and there will exist a global empire that enforces international law and squashes any dissenters.

This popular view of Kojève is only correct up to a certain point, as it misses some of the subtle nuance of his thought. His theories on international law and the death of Nation-States are not just vaguely hinted at in his *Introduction à la lecture de Hegel,* but are given thorough examination in other treatises dedicated exclusively to the topic. Though the scope of this chapter limits the possibility of examining them in depth, it is important to know that in works such as *La Notion de l'Autorité, Outline of a Phenomenology of Right*, and the essay "Latin Empire: Sketch of a Doctrine of French Policy" Kojève makes a rather convincing case for what seem at first glance outrageous positions. In the following analysis, I am heavily indebted to James Nichol's masterly study of Kojève's life and thought in *Alexandre Kojève: Wisdom at the End of History*.

To the surprise of many, Kojève in fact *did not believe* in the basic inevitability of the Universal and Homogeneous State. Though he thought its emergence extremely likely, given the then-current trajectory of global economic and political activity, it was by no means certain. For Kojève, the historical process is *highly contingent*. Human beings are essentially free, and so the future course of history is impossible to know with certainty. For instance, Kojève admits that he does not know at this point in the historical process whether the future belongs to right-wing or left-wing Hegelians. However, his thesis holds that *defensible* political and economic policies all tend toward the same end state, whose foundation was laid in 1806 with the Napoleonic reforms.[3] Though conceding that the future is indeed contingent in many ways, he argues that all actions of which a *reasonable account* can be given lead in the same direction—toward a near synthesis of the right-wing and left-wing Hegelian positions.

Nichols argues that, for Kojève, rationality cannot abolish all contingency. Using persuasion, it can dissuade one from irrational courses of action, but it cannot force action. It cannot guarantee that human beings will not choose quite obviously irrational paths that would cause the historical process to retrogress to an earlier stage of development. As an example, Kojève observes that German National Socialism was such an irrational retrogressive movement. It attempted to resurrect the political Nation-State in an epoch when only multicultural empires could hold sway. The existence of National Socialism was, therefore, a contradiction. It attempted to build a *global* empire after the model of a Nation-State. This attempt would only lead to its self-destruction, since conquered territories would not possibly be willing to adopt the Nazis' nationalistic platform. As Nichols notes,

> The inescapable fact is that neither philosophy nor wisdom can now or ever refute the most stubborn irrationality. The most wisdom can do is to enable us to understand the whole, but not necessarily to dominate it so thoroughly as to conquer all contingency. But granting this limitation, one can nonetheless say that modern rationality does tend to provide more powerful arms on the side of reason than the unending debate between opposed positions in the premodern tradition of western philosophy ever did.[4]

As Nation-States—such as Great Britain, the Soviet Union, and America—gradually metamorphosed into multicultural empires spanning several continents, technological and military capacity underwent revolutionary changes as well. This military capacity allowed allied powers to defeat Germany and Japan in the Second World War. In Kojève's view, the latter two Nations stubbornly held on to an irrational and retrogressive political and economic platform. The allied powers thus literally had to *force them to be rational*. The greatest outcome of World War II was, therefore, that it brought the backward civilizations of the world into line with the most advanced European historical positions.[5]

According to Nichols, Kojève admits he does not know exactly how the details of the future course of history will work themselves out. However, he quite confidently extrapolates two trends: first, the fact that political entities are controlling more and more of the globe and, second, the reality that technological and military capacity enables these larger political entities to maintain control over these larger territories. The two dominant political empires during Kojève's lifetime were the Anglo-American and Soviet-Slavic.[6] Like Heidegger, he believed that the two empires were essentially the same, though he predicted America would eventually persevere in the struggle between the two.

For Kojève, its ability to synthesize communism and capitalism was the major reason why America, and not the Soviet Union, heralded the future course of historical development and perhaps the final political configuration at the End of History. Marx was correct in his diagnosis of the fundamental flaw in the capitalist order—namely, that it encouraged technological progress but failed to share the fruits of that progress with the vast majority of the population. However, he was wrong about one important thing: "He thought it impossible that Capitalists could ever have the foresight necessary to see that unfettered worker exploitation was on a path to revolutionary self-destruction."[7] He thought that only violent revolution could fundamentally change the capitalist order.

Kojève was skeptical of this traditional Marxist view. He argues instead that the uniquely American configuration of capitalism—which he playfully calls "Fordist capitalism"—succeeds in overcoming Marxist critiques because it attempts to maximize the purchasing power of workers. For Kojève, Henry Ford was the one true exemplar of Marxism in the twentieth century, because he worked to solve the problem of capitalism that Marx correctly diagnosed. He paid his workers more than the market wage required. He donated a large sum of money to the state of Massachusetts to build a superhighway. And he engaged in other great acts of charity that won him the respect of rich and poor alike. He understood that "a poor customer is a bad customer," and so attempted to raise the purchasing power of his workers. The Socialism of the Soviet Union was basically like the pre-Fordized capitalism, except the State, instead of private capitalists, invested the surplus value not shared with workers.[8] This focus on working-class purchasing power, Kojève predicted, was the chief reason America would eventually overtake the Soviet Union as global economic and political leader. It understood this "Fordist" principle on a large scale.[9]

Yet Kojève argues that despite its appearance as an easy resolution to the capitalist predicament, "Fordist capitalism" still carries with it a major contradiction possibly hindering the achievements of the End of History. Although the Fordist paradigm definitely seems to work within a single nation, one could very well wonder how it could be applied in a globalized economy, where workers and investors often live on opposite sides of the globe. As Zizek has observed, in a postcolonial age marked by globalization, has not the problem of worker exploitation simply been shifted outside the perspective of most First-World inhabitants, so that they neither know nor see the effects of the real exploitation that occurs in Asia, Africa, and South America, the former colonies of Europe?[10] Kojève must address this problem if the End of History is going to be anything but empty rhetoric.

Kojève's solution involves a "Fordizing" not only of national economies but of the entire global market. As Nichols summarizes his argument,

> In the long run, with a truly global economy, a political-economic structure that continues to leave the majority poor while providing further constant enrichment to a minority will not be sustainable. Accordingly, just as certain capitalists before . . . so statesmen and economic leaders today should address the fundamental problem of the global political economy, colonialism. . . . *The task of political economy globally understood, therefore, is to bring it about that all the people of the world share in the fruits of technological progress.*[11]

Industrialized nations will accomplish this in three ways: first, they can work to make trade agreements according to which they would jointly bind themselves to paying higher prices for the products, especially raw materials, which they import from underdeveloped countries. Second, they can give indirect financial aid to these countries through international organizations. Finally, particular countries—most importantly, the former imperialist countries—could give direct aid to former colonies.[12] Colonialism needs to change just as old-style capitalism needed to change. Specifically, it needs to change from what Nichols calls a "taking-colonialism" to a "giving-colonialism," which would return the surplus value produced in the industrialized nations back to the poorer areas of the world. These goals were fundamental for Kojève's work at the French Ministry of Finance.[13]

With all of the contradictions and troubles of old-style capitalism overcome, at least theoretically, global economic leaders from the outset would take away the emotional and economic drivers of revolutionary action on the part of the poor and marginalized. All striving after freedom and equality would ultimately be redeemed, setting the stage for the final political and economic arrangements at the End of History. As the world stood at the time of Kojève's death, the Slavo-Soviet sphere of influence was bound to give way to the Anglo-American, which had, in Kojève's mind, achieved the final stage of Marxist development and the "animalization" of man.[14] Though many minor details were left to be worked out, the broad outline and main features of the final stage of historical development were clearly visible.

NOTES

1. See Shadia B. Drury, *Alexandre Kojève: The Roots of Postmodern Politics* (New York: St. Martin's Press, 1994). I will explain Drury's thesis in more detail later on in this chapter.

2. It is a little-known fact among scholars that Kojève was rather explicit about how he *deliberately* misinterpreted Hegel. Because, as he saw it, all political movements since 1806 have been fundamentally affected by Hegelianism, the work of an interpreter of Hegel takes on the meaning of *political propaganda*. As Kojève comments, "It may be that, in fact, the future of the world, and therefore the meaning of the present and the significance of the past, depend, in the final analysis, on the way in which the Hegelian writings are interpreted today" ("Hegel, Marx, and Christianity," quoted in James Nichols, *Alexandre Kojève: Wisdom at the End of History* [Lanham: Rowman and Littlefield Publishers, 2007] 82).

3. Ibid.

4. Nichols, *Alexandre Kojève: Wisdom at the End of History*, 95–96.

5. Ibid., 84.

6. It is interesting to note that Kojève hoped that a third, Mediterranean or European empire would emerge led by France. This "Latin Empire," consisting of France, Spain, Italy, and their North African colonies would stand between the Anglo-American and Slavo-Soviet empires in several different ways. First, it would provide a sort of military check to American and Soviet dominance. Second, and perhaps most importantly, it would prevent European culture from being destroyed by increasing "Americanization." Europe, more than the United States, has cultivated the leisure activities, arts, and cultures to a high degree. The purpose of this European block would be to preserve culture at the End of History. This hope was one of the reasons for his tireless efforts in laying the groundwork for the European Union. See "Latin Empire: Sketch of a Doctrine of French Policy," (August 27, 1945), tr. Erik de Vries in *Policy Review* (2004).

7. Nichols, *Alexandre Kojève*, 90.

8. Ibid.

9. Ibid, 91.

10. This is the subject of Lenin's very influential treatise "Imperialism, the Highest Stage of Capitalism," in which he argues that Capitalism has grown into a worldwide system of colonial oppression and of the financial strangulation of the overwhelming

majority of the population of the world by a handful of "advanced" countries (*The Lenin Anthology,* ed. and tr. Robert C. Tucker [New York: W. W. Norton and Company, 1975], 207). Kojève's assessment of the global economic and political order is highly Leninist in flavor, though his solution to Colonialism is more pacifistic than Lenin's and mainstream Marxists'.

11. Nichols, *Alexandre Kojève,* 92. My emphasis.

12. Ibid.

13. Ibid., 93.

14. Undeniably influenced by Nietzsche's portrayal of the "Last Man," Kojève believed that one of the distinctive characteristics of the End of History was that human beings would return to a sort of prehuman—one might say, animalistic—state in which the most important ends desired and achieved would be primarily bodily in character. Significantly, that quality of humanity which kick-started the historical development—namely, the desire for recognition and the willingness to die for it—would dissolve away. Among the many ironies of the end of history, the fact that "universal recognition" will be accorded to human beings who are no longer willing to die for it is perhaps the greatest.

Chapter 20

How Valid Are Kojève's Observations on the Modern World?

Kojève's views have drawn criticism from all corners of the political spectrum, from Marxists who would argue that his "Fordist Capitalism" is nothing but what Marx called the mentality of the "Petty Bourgeois," to conservatives like Strauss and his progeny who claim that the homogenization of man would spell the destruction of mankind and a radical distortion of the nature and possibility of philosophy.[1] But it is undeniable that there is something enticing about Kojève's picture of modernity. Though it appears exaggerated at first glance, one can certainly recognize its main features in the world around us. Technology has a long way to go, but it truly is rendering our lives more calculated, rigid, and homogenized. It really does make communication with anyone on earth more universally accessible. Modern economic policies have been the deathblow to native ethnic cultures. It seems wherever one goes, one will find human beings wearing similar clothes, using the same technology, and behaving in the same "animalistic" way. Yet as is also very clear, something very important seems to have been lost in the modern world. Especially for those who have studied Hegel's political thought closely, one can't help but see that something vital has gone awry, that somewhere along the line the train has derailed.

Though she may be wrong on some particulars, Shadia B. Drury has done a magnificent job tracing the lines of Kojève's influence on the French and American intellectual scenes in the middle part of the twentieth century. Her basic thesis is that the postmodern reaction to the cold, lifeless, tyrannical rationality of modernity—in which everything is quantified, homogenized, and ordered—as well as the postmodern nostalgia for transgression, passion, unreason, and diversity, is not so much a reaction to modernity *per se* but to Kojève's account of the modern world. Unlike Kojève's version, Hegel's modernity is "rationalistic without being cold, soulless, and indifferent. Hegel's rationalism has an emotional or passionate dimension. In contrast, Kojève's thinking is not only materialistic and anthropocentric but also dualistic, romantic, and irrational."[2] The problem with Kojève is that he

> replaces the dialectic with an extreme dualism between reason and passion, femininity and masculinity, necessity and freedom, discipline and spontaneity. And while he follows Hegel in thinking that reason is bound to triumph in history, it is a cold, soulless, instrumental, and heartless rationalism that conquers the world.[3]

Authors such as Foucault and Bataille simply opt for the other half of Kojève's dualisms. They choose particularity over universality, diversity over homogenization, passion over cold rationality, and transgression or spontaneity over rigid discipline. Their work is thus fundamentally linked to Kojève's view of modernity, even as they react against it.

But how did Kojève come to hold these views on the modern world? If Drury is correct, and Kojève's perspective one-dimensionally overlooks certain key features of human existence, then, where is his fatal flaw? To answer this, it will be necessary to understand not only his views on the present and future course of history, but also mankind's past. In true Hegelian fashion, Kojève holds that man is a historical being, one whose conception of himself and the world around him changes depending on the historical epoch in which he lives. Significantly, on this score Kojève differs from Hegel in one important respect: in more of a Marxist vein, he maintains that these different viewpoints on himself and his world are merely some sort of denial or theoretical superstructure covering over his underlying essence. Despite appearances to the contrary, human beings, for Kojève, do indeed have a "nature" or "essence" that must be worked out and affirmed through the historical process. This view leads him to commit one of the most striking errors in the entirety of the *Introduction*, which has led Drury to claim that Kojève's philosophy is a "parody of essentialism": his misleading use of the Master-Slave dialectic as the key to the historical course and man *qua* man. Dale, Nichols, and Drury, among others, have emphasized this key detail. One of the consequences of this misuse is that it allows history to now be interpreted as the gradual overcoming of the master by the slave. For the historical course to be complete, a violent revolution is necessary in which the slaves take up once again the life-or-death struggle they originally repudiated. As Nichols indicates, "This account of the historical course has a decidedly Marxist flavor to it insofar as it emphasizes the workers (=slaves) as the active agents of historical advance."[4] What serves as a very minor stage in the Hegelian account of history becomes the cornerstone of the Kojèvian one.

One of the problems with this use of the *Herr-Knecht* (Master-Slave) dialectic is that, as Drury points out, based upon Kojève's presuppositions alone, there is no real reason why history must progress beyond this elemental stage—in Kojève's mind, the age of pagan Greeks. If the situation of the Master is "tragic" to the extent that he *seeks* recognition through conquest and subordinating others to his will but can only *find* satisfaction through the mutual recognition of an equal, then Kojève's association of the age of Mastery with the world of Greek antiquity would be misguided. As Drury comments, "By equating mastery with the pagan state and with the conditions of social life and mutual recognition, Kojève undermines his claim that mastery ends in an 'impasse.' In other words, the master's situation loses the tragic quality it had in the Hegelian account. Even though the admiration of his slaves is not enough for him, the master is recognized by his fellow masters. Moreover, the act of conquest satisfies his negativity and affirms his freedom as a creative being."[5] In addition, saying that the Master no longer needs to "act" in the genuinely human sense once he has made his conquests would also be misleading. Mastery is never something that can be achieved and relied on once and for all, since as long as slavery exists the master's position is insecure. The slaves can rise up at a time and place of their choosing, effectively restarting this elemental stage of the historical process.[6]

Eric Michael Dale agrees with Drury that Kojève, unlike Hegel, mistakenly associated this dialectic with a concrete historical society. Instead of being the beginning that provides the *telos* for the historical dialectic, the Master-Slave dialectic should be understood as the

> start of a long historical process of striving for freedom, which is still ongoing and *must remain a futural project* according to the Hegelian account of history. The *Herr-Knecht* dialectic is a phenomenological model of how that striving takes place, not an actual description of an activity in time which can be tied to any given historical occurrence.[7]

When Kojève links this dialectic to the world of antiquity, he makes a move Hegel never makes, thereby allowing for its later improper use as the sign of the beginning and end of history. Kojève introduces a paradigmatic example into a process of pragmatic events, and subsequently blurs the lines between them.

Dale continues:

> Alexandre Kojève's reading is a good example of what happens when the *Phenomenology of Spirit* is given too much emphasis in any exegesis of Hegel. To base the entirety of Hegelian philosophy of history on the opening third of Hegel's first major publication, and to overlook the role of history, not only in

the remainder of the book, but in the rest of Hegel's output, is to paint a highly idiosyncratic picture of Hegel's idea of history.[8]

Neither Hegel's history nor the actual historical course begins with "*la lutte entre les maîtres et les esclaves* (the fight between masters and slaves)." One could critique Kojève from two angles. On the one hand, a close reading of the *Phenomenology of Spirit* shows that Hegel's so-called history of Spirit begins with the problems surrounding *sense-certainty*—for instance, the inadequacy of sense-data to get at the intelligibility of things, along with the consequences of this failure. Couldn't one thus object against Kojève's interpretation that the problem of the human relationship to Being is both prior to and more important than the human desire for recognition? Put another way, Hegel's opening chapter in the *Phenomenology of Spirit* on "sense-certainty" demonstrates how the rational contemplation of particular concretely existing objects logically entails the all-encompassing notion of Being. In contemplating the particular, we are oriented toward the universal. Human beings, therefore, prior to anything else, *have a transcendent orientation*. On the other hand, from a purely anthropological or historical standpoint—leaving aside what Hegel thought—it seems that Kojève seriously simplifies mankind's historical origins. Psychologists and anthropologists are still plumbing the deepest depths of the human psyche, and the primordial origins of these mysteries seem to go back tens of thousands of years. To reduce the complexity of the human psyche and all of its desires and emotions to the simple "*désir pour la reconnaissance* (desire for recognition)," is to fundamentally distort the human subject and to profoundly misunderstand the society of which he is a part. Though this desire is indeed central in Hegel's views of humanity and human society, it is not humanity's sole desire and must be understood in light of many other aspects of his thought.

If one believes that history is the gradual overcoming of the master by the slave, and that the greatest accomplishment human societies can strive for is a basic recognition of these slaves in their animalistic bodily being, then the floodgates are opened for some very outlandish views on politics and culture. If, on top of this, one believes that to fully overcome the masters of history, the slaves must finally confront death in all of its dark brutality, then permission is granted for some of the most atrocious activities history has ever witnessed. What may result is what Drury calls Kojève's "terrorist conception of history." It is well known that Kojève admired Stalin and thought that he and Stalin were linked just as Hegel and Napoleon were linked. But it must be understood that "Kojève did not admire Stalin simply because he used horrific tactics to accomplish justifiable political goals. Terror was not just the price of Stalin's achievements. Rather, terror was *integral to* the accomplishments themselves." Terror was not just a means to an end, in Kojève's view, but part of the end itself. If, as he argues, the slaves must accept their mortality and confront death "voluntarily" by putting aside biological necessity, then terror itself, simply for the sake of terror, becomes a goal to be sought.[9] At the End of History, the slaves will be willing to do what is most properly human in Kojève's eyes—die voluntarily for the sake of media and societal recognition.

Any concrete political society that has terror and voluntary death as its basis would be neither a healthy one nor one that allows for human flourishing. From a truly Hegelian perspective, as well as from a general commonsense one, Kojève's views on voluntary death appear patently absurd, opening up the possibility for the worst sorts of atrocities and a stifling of the highest human qualities and aspirations. As we will see, Hegel's "rational" political order has nothing at all to do with Kojève's cold, calculating, universal, and homogeneous state. Rationality, life, and human flourishing all go hand in hand. One might even say that, for Hegel, a society is rational to the extent that it allows for human flourishing in all its forms—philosophic, artistic, moral, and religious. The human being in this rational State is a far cry from Kojève's animalistic Last Man.

What about Kojève's views on the modern world's economic and technological trajectory? Is he not correct that a more globalized world becomes more homogenized and universal, and that technological progress renders national, cultural, and social differences obsolete? Here again, Kojève's portrait is enticing yet incomplete. From both a Hegelian and commonsense theoretical perspective, the future course of technological and economic progress is uncertain, and there is really no inherent reason why progress must continue indefinitely in a unilinear fashion. Indeed, as many geopolitical forecasters are beginning to argue, the current economic and technological *status quo* seems likely to enter into what Bernard Lonergan calls the "Shorter and Longer cycles of decline."[10] Lonergan's work may also help us to understand why continual progress in technology and economics is far from certain and indeed may be reversing. Kojève's analysis of the contemporary world focuses less on the fact that concrete historical actors must have the insights necessary to keep economic and technological progress going, and more on general trends and *a priori* assumptions about current trajectories. Unlike in Kojève's *a priori* account of the future, Lonergan emphasizes the consciously acting human subjects who must make decisions that affect the future course of history.

According to Lonergan, it is only through appropriating ourselves as knowers that we become the attentive, intelligent, reasonable, and responsible historical actors of the future, who will not be satisfied with short-term solutions to historical crises posing long-term threats. Only in this way can indefinite political and technological progress be possible. Yet unfortunately, the world's political leaders will most likely not be willing to take this decisive step. Myriad forms of bias and the perceived need to win elections will ensure that actions aimed at resolving long-term issues will be purely symbolic and largely ineffective. They will shift the responsibility to future generations. Indeed, one might even say *that the conscious or unconscious belief that history is over constitutes one of the worst forms of contemporary political bias that, ironically, will ensure history will continue developing in new and unforeseen ways.* The unexamined dogma that democracy and an ever-expanding array of human rights are universally valid for all human beings might just succeed in sufficiently antagonizing those societies and cultures not abiding by these ideals to ensure an organized opposition to them. What is more, it is one thing to say that contemporary political societies have successfully overcome some of the worst crises hitherto known to man by means of the diplomacy international law makes possible and the fruits of technological progress. It is quite another thing to say that humans will continue indefinitely to overcome these crises. For concrete acting humans, with all sorts of shortcomings and biases, need to have the concrete insights enabling them to confront political, environmental, and economic crises. Tragically, we do not always have the insights political reality requires. Kojève assumes that the technological apparatus making a global economic and political situation possible will somehow maintain itself after the world's population has metamorphosed into a horde of Last Men. But Lonergan would ask the simple questions: Who will operate this technology? Which technicians? Will the leaders of the Universal and Homogeneous State not make some basic miscalculations that will throw the entire world order out of balance? Even those with the purest of intentions, who have completely unleashed what Lonergan calls "the pure disinterested desire to know," might find that accounting for all of the variables and conditions that determine scenarios in history is simply beyond their intellectual or computing capacities, that the structure of human society and its complex web of interrelations is much too multifaceted and blurry. How, therefore, would it be possible for Kojève's universal and homogeneous man, who lives in a state of perpetual comfort, to make the prudent political and economic decisions that would perpetuate the world order at the end of history?

As I will explain in more detail, authentic Hegelians might also call into question Kojève's presuppositions about the unfolding of history and the role of historical actors in it. The most apparent objection stems from an insight into what Hegel calls the "Cunning of Reason"—*der List der Vernuft.* This model for understanding history is premised on the empirical truth that no historical actor—not even the great world-historical individuals who fully understand their respective epochs and help to advance its transition to a higher stage of development—can be fully conscious of the full ramifications of their deeds. Because, for Hegel, the universal must be actualized in the particular, "human actions produce additional results, beyond their immediate purpose and attainment, beyond their immediate knowledge and desire. They gratify their own interests; but something more is thereby accomplished, which is latent in the action though not present in their consciousness and not included in their design."[11] Actions as simple as going to the grocery store to feed one's family or buying clothes from a department store have far-reaching economic and political consequences that are not completely visible from the perspective of the actor. These simple acts create the conditions for the possibility of certain economic and political orders. They extend beyond the agent himself to other individuals living in far corners of the globe. They help to perpetuate or destroy certain economic or technological orders that depend upon these actors for their survival.

This hypothesis becomes even more convincing when one looks at global politics and the actors who have the capacity to change the course of history on a large scale. Who knew, for instance, that the arming and training of the Mujahideen during the 1988 Soviet war in Afghanistan to confront the spread of Soviet Communism would end up backfiring on the United States? Though this policy may have been the most prudent geopolitical strategy at the time, it contained latent within itself certain possibilities for which nobody could successfully account. Hegel himself often points to the events of the French Revolution to illustrate this principle. Not only did tyranny, inequality, and destruction result from a genuine desire for *liberté, égalité, et fraternité,* but all the revolutionaries' efforts to stamp out the effects of the Catholic faith in their culture only led to a resurgence of religion in the Romantic era. According to Hegel, there was no way these historical actors could have been aware of their actions' long-term effects. The dynamic structure of history is such that nobody, not even the best and most astute minds of the time, can forecast the future.

Whether we analyze the French Revolution or the wars in Afghanistan, the Hegelian hypothesis of the cunning of reason maintains that there is something about historical development, and the various ways humans contribute to it, that eludes our grasp and refuses to be pinned down by any classical or modern statistical laws. It affirms that no matter how hard one tries, no matter how insightful one is, there is always something in our actions that slips away from us, making it impossible to ever fully account for the complete set of ramifications and possibilities they open up.[12] Hegel would state that all of the prior conditions that must be met to give rise to a higher or novel world-order can only be recognized *retrospectively*, after the new world-order has already emerged. For Hegel, this is what it means for individuals and societies to "posit their presuppositions." These presuppositions—or, as Lonergan, would later call them, historical preconditions—can only be recognized or posited after the later historical reality that depends on them has appeared. For Hegel, it is impossible, therefore, based on the current data of a world situation, to look to the future and effectively predict what will occur.

Hegel's philosophy of history is oriented toward the present and past, not the future. This orientation is one of the major sticking points for Kojève, who, following Marx, believed philosophy's current vocation is to *shape history rather than understand it*. In effect, they believed it had already been understood. Marx, indeed, emphasized, to the almost total exclusion of retrospective theorizing, forward-looking Praxis. This is because, as he would have it, the truth only emerges through our work on objects—in this case, the object of the *Bürgerlichgesellschaft* or Bourgeois civil society and the modes of production that render it possible. Slavoj Zizek clearly summarizes the basic differences between the Hegelian and Marxist views of the relationship between human actors and the history they create:

> Hegel is, of course, fully aware of the fact that our thinking wants to "jump ahead of its time" and project a future; his point is that such thinking is always and by definition "ideological," mistaken: its intervention into Being generates something unexpected, totally different from what was projected. Therein resides the lesson of the French Revolution: the pure thought of universal equality and freedom, imposing itself onto social Being, generated Terror. Marx's counter-argument here is that his revolutionary theory is not a utopian projection into the future: it merely extrapolates tendencies and possibilities from the antagonisms of the present.[13]

If, for Hegel, we can only discover the intelligibility of a given world-order retrospectively, after it has already emerged, then there can be no such Praxis that would succeed in shaping history along desired or projected lines. Kojève, on the contrary, appears to be more in line with Marx's position that human agents are capable of self-consciously appropriating their capacity to steer history in directions dictated by the possibilities buried within the present. These actors must rely on the theorist's abilities to unearth these buried and concealed possibilities so that their actions do not become mere guesses leading to dead ends. While Kojève is certainly not advocating revolutionary action to bring these latent possibilities to light—since, for him, Fordist capitalism has made revolution unnecessary—he does believe that forward-looking praxis is not only possible at the end of history, but a necessary logical outcome of philosophy's completion. Kojève's work in the French Ministry of Finance stands in stark contrast to the revolutionary praxis Marx advocates.

We are left with two radically opposed positions on the possibility of consciously shaping history: the Marxist-Kojèvian and the Hegelian. Which is more convincing? If we are to get at an adequate understanding of the possibility that history has ended or will end in the way Kojève claims, it seems we must look further into the possibility of a Praxis that would shape history along desired lines. We must do this in light of a broader account of how human beings act in the world. It is here that Bernard Lonergan's theory of emergent probability can fill in the gaps left by Kojève and Marx. This theory, I believe, functions as a more differentiated account of Hegel's cunning of reason and reveals the mechanisms behind it. I believe Lonergan's account of modern politics to be the most sober, convincing, and, ultimately, most in line with Hegel's own position. First, because of what he calls the individual, group, and general biases of common sense operative in all communities, new social situations will arise to which a responsible and adequate response will be unlikely—say, for instance, insufficient preparation for an environmental catastrophe or failure to properly weigh the threat posed by a foreign enemy. These biases render human agents myopic, egotistical, and careless. Human agents will almost inevitably fail to recognize the full set of conditions giving rise to a desired set of circumstances or those maintaining one already in effect. Let's say, for example, there is some desired circumstance X—what Lonergan would call a scheme of recurrence. X has its necessary preconditions a, b, c, d, e, f, g, and h. Each of these preconditions depends upon the person acting as the effective agent capable of recognizing their necessity and working to bring them into existence. If this person, as a historical actor, fails to account for even one of these conditions, a completely unintended historical reality may result—say, circumstance Y. Y, from the perspective of the actor, is the complete opposite of what he had intended. It is important to emphasize that the possibility a given historical actor will overlook one of these conditions is itself ruled by other preconditions.[14] Various factors—such as the individual's level of intelligence, purity of motives, and so on—come together to determine whether it will be probable or unlikely he will have insight into all of these necessary conditions.

For Lonergan, it is apparent humans can, under certain circumstances, shape their own lives in accordance with their desires. We can see this shaping on a large scale among healthy individuals living in healthy political societies. The individual sets goals—for example, to lose weight or finish a degree—and accomplishes them. There are extraneous factors and conditions that may affect the probability a given person will accomplish these goals. Maybe he has genetic or economic limitations, or family responsibilities. But, for the most part, individuals can and do achieve their goals. For Lonergan, to say there is a "cunning of reason" operative in *all* of our actions, whether on an individual or political level, is empirically false, and simply overlooks the way conscious choice is actually operative in our lives. Lonergan explains Hegel's cunning of reason in a different way. While it is certainly true that many if not most of our actions result in unintended consequences, we can account for this occurrence rather simply by acknowledging the ubiquitous tendency among humans to *overlook* factors that might influence a desired chain of causality. If, as I mentioned above, a person desires X but he fails to account for c, then it might appear as if there was some "cunning of reason" working behind his back. In reality, the "cunning of reason" boils down to the statistical probability that a person will overlook a necessary condition for a desired historical reality. For Lonergan, we can trace this probability back to the impact of the various biases operative in the intellectual processes of the human person. It is not the case that politicians and world leaders do not see the latent possibilities in their actions because history is a mysterious trickster. Rather, they do not see them because they fail to apperceive the world clearly, as it is in its current state of development.

Whereas Hegel looks upon history from the bird's-eye view of the owl of Minerva, and sees these unintended consequences retrospectively from a distance, Lonergan focuses upon the concrete human actor as he has insights into, judges, and acts upon concrete situations. He asks, why did *this* person forget to account for *this* variable in this situation? Why did that person overlook one of the necessary conditions for a desired outcome? These questions usually have very clear answers, stemming from a defect in the cognitional processes of the individual in question. The United States on September 11, for instance, was not a victim of history's revenge coming back to haunt it after aiding its future attackers in the Soviet-Afghan War. Instead, there was a very palpable oversight involved, perhaps of the extent to which Pashtun Muslims felt their culture being influenced by Western ideas, or of the extreme views held by what would come to be known as Al-Qaida. It is even probable the CIA knew the potential risks involved in helping these actors. Likewise, the actors in the French Revolution were not destined to create the Reign of Terror because history worked to spite them. Rather, they simply failed to see that Freedom requires intermediary institutional structures between the so-called "people" and the will of a ruler. Hegel's "cunning of reason" appears here in a new light, as an oversight of a necessary condition for a desired historical reality.

So where might Kojève's End of History thesis fit in here? What this thesis amounts to is the *belief* that a set of economic, technological, political, and cultural circumstances will *maintain themselves indefinitely*. In Kojève's view, history has reached a point where economic and political systems can *maintain themselves,* independent of the conscious actions of individual human beings. For Kojève, "Fordist" capitalism is the most rational economic order because it simultaneously depends on, thrives off, and fosters real human needs and desires. A global international empire is inevitable because, in an age of nuclear weapons, no rational country would risk possible destruction when diplomacy and compromise are possible. Likewise, indefinite technological progress is necessary because it is funded by what it produces—namely, food, power, shelter, and entertainment—and its progress makes even greater future progress possible. Technological advances allow for greater scientific advances, which, in turn, allow for further technological advances. Finally, technology, like the modern economic order, feeds real human needs and desires. In sum, all of these systems *perpetuate their own conditions,* and thus rely much less on conscious human agents for their existence. What this means, for Kojève, is that history as the product of human negative activity—*l'action négatrice*—will end.

From Hegel's and Lonergan's perspective, Kojève's theory contains many flaws. One could ask a series of rather commonsense questions that might succeed in undermining it: Does Fordist capitalism depend on the owners of the means of production having the insight that they should pay workers more to maximize their buying power? Hasn't this reality changed in an age of publicly owned companies catering to their investors who only care about short-term profits? Even if one generation of business leaders follow the Fordist capitalism paradigm, does this guarantee that their successors will? Furthermore, is it always necessary that the workers themselves will choose to reinvest their money in the Fordist economy? Could they not save or spend it elsewhere? In regard to Kojève's belief that unending technological progress is inevitable, could one also not ask about the technicians and scientists who must have the insights into how best to use the technology they have created? Are not intelligent and educated technicians required who can fix it when it breaks? If technology grows more and more complex, will there not be fewer people who can understand how it works and therefore fix or put it to proper use? If, as in Rousseau's critique of the modern world, one of the consequences of technological progress is that it renders humans more enslaved to technology, what would happen if one of the conditions upon which a nation's technological apparatuses depends were to be destroyed—for instance, in a terrorist attack on the power grid or a large-scale environmental catastrophe? Would this not plunge societies back into the maelstrom of history? With respect to the international law supposedly imposed at the end of history, what is to prevent a nation's leaders from engaging in suicidal warfare? If the twentieth century is any indication, leaders willing to bring their entire nation over the precipice are not rare. Moreover, even if it can be assumed that nations still exist and strive rationally to maximize the quality of life for their populations, is it not likely that at least one of the leaders of these nations will miscalculate the costs/benefits of a war that could possibly lead to greater economic and political influence? Isn't there a risk and reward associated with every conflict? And if a leader believes that the reward of conquering a territory, establishing regional or global hegemony, or appropriating the resources of another nation outweighs the risk of engaging in armed conflict, will they not do it? Contemporary Sino-U.S relations instantiate many of the questions above. How these two countries answer them will in large measure determine the trajectory of the twenty-first century, and decide whether Kojève's End of History is a chimera masking balance-of-power politics or a universally relatable standard for all countries to follow.

NOTES

1. See Leo Strauss's debate with Kojève, in *On Tyranny*, eds. Victor Gourevitch and Michael S. Roth (Chicago: University of Chicago Press, 2000).

2. Shadia B. Drury, *Alexandre Kojève: The Roots of Postmodern Politics* (New York: St. Martin's Press, 1994), 15.

3. Ibid.

4. James H. Nichols, *Alexandre Kojève: Wisdom at the End of History* (Lanham: Rowman and Littlefield Publishers, 2007), 26.

5. Drury, *Alexandre Kojève: The Roots of Postmodern Politics*, 22.

6. Ibid.

7. Eric Michael Dale, *Hegel, the End of History, and the Future* (Cambridge: Cambridge University Press, 2014), 106.

8. Ibid.

9. Drury, *Alexandre Kojève: The Roots of Postmodern Politics*, 37.

10. See Peter Ziehen, *Disunited Nations* (New York: HarperCollins, 2020).

11. G. W. F. Hegel, *Introduction to the Lectures on the Philosophy of History*, tr. Robert S. Hartman (Englewood Cliffs: Prentice Hall Publishing, 1953), 35.

12. This is the primary reason why Hegel acknowledges the need for a community of confession and forgiveness. These human actions are the only ones that can heal the wounds opened up by the unpredictability of our actions. See section on "Morality" in the *Phenomenology of Spirit*, 405.

13. Slavoj Zizek, *Less Than Nothing: Hegel and the Shadow of Dialectical Materialism* (New York: Verso Publishing, 2012), 259–260.

14. Bernard Lonergan, *Insight* (Toronto: University of Toronto Press, 1992), 236.

Chapter 21

Why Hegel's Rational State Is Neither Universal Nor Homogeneous

In all fairness to Kojève and those influenced by him, interpreting Hegel's stance on philosophical issues is one of the most difficult tasks a scholar can undertake. It is much easier to point out the flaws in another's analyses than to tease out one's own coherent perspective on Hegel. With that said, the following section will only present Hegel's stance on political issues bearing on the End of History idea. In lieu of arguing that Hegel's work suggests one single interpretation one must hold in order to be a true Hegelian, I will suggest there exists a fundamental (and deliberate?) ambiguity in Hegel's comments on the End of History that could give rise to two viable interpretations. These are positions (2)—that the End of History means the *teleological completion* of history—and (4)—that the End of History means the completion or end of an *historical era*, but not necessarily of "history" strictly speaking. Both positions have their advocates; both are supported by Hegel's texts; and both stand up to theoretical criticism.

The one thing a Hegel scholar can be certain of is that Hegel does not hold position (1). First, he would fundamentally disagree with Kojève's belief in the possibility of a universal global empire. He says as much explicitly in just about all of his published political writings. Just before the section on *Das äußere Staatsrecht* (International Relations) in the *Philosophy of Right*, Hegel makes a convincing case for why a global empire is neither desirable nor possible. The first part of his argument suggests that any peaceful *status quo* a universal empire could achieve would very quickly undermine itself. As Hegel comments, "In peace, the bounds of civil life are extended, all its spheres become firmly established, and in the long run, people become stuck in their ways. Their particular characteristics become increasingly rigid and ossified. But the unity of the body is essential to its health, and if its parts grow internally hard, the result is death."[1] Hegel is not here celebrating war and destruction for its own sake—as sometimes it seems Kojève does. Rather, he is soberly pointing to an undeniable fact of history. When a nation's population has become too accustomed to peace and prosperity, citizens are typically less willing to risk life, and thus defensive, preemptive, and offensive wars become harder to wage. Individuals focus almost exclusively on selfish needs in their Civil Society pursuits. The spirit of the nation—that which binds it together so that it can execute common goals—will begin to decay and thus put the very survival of the nation in jeopardy.

Central here is Hegel's basic distinction between the State and Civil Society. Importantly, Kojève never makes this distinction. For Hegel, Civil Society is that sphere of political order that caters to and allows for men's selfish pursuits. It allows them to establish careers, make money, acquire property, and use it however they wish. It is what we might call today the "economic sphere" of a political order. Individuality here is king. While the family ties one to other human beings and morally obligates one to love and care for them, Civil Society allows one to exist merely for oneself or to satisfy the needs of family dependents. Yet since the State as a whole *preserves* Civil Society—insofar as it procures natural resources, defends it against foreign invaders, provides a police force to ensure peaceful and lawful intercourse, and most importantly articulates laws by which humans exchange goods on the market with minimal disputes—it carries a higher ethical duty than Civil Society. The State, for Hegel, is where Ethical life (*Sittlichkeit*) can be seen in full force. Everything within a given political order—families, occupations, corporations, economic activity—depend entirely on the State for their existence and health.

When Kojève, on the other hand, speaks of the universal and homogeneous State, he has reduced the State to a mere means of preserving men and catering to their animalistic urges. While the State, for him, does indeed "recognize" each individual person in their sheer "being," this recognition is accorded only for their bodily or animalistic existence—that part which desires bodily satisfaction—and not for any of their higher spiritual capacities. This view seems to blur the distinction between the State and Civil Society. If the State at the End of History has no other purpose than to properly "manage" and administer human bodily satisfactions—Kojève himself asserts that at the End of History Politics properly understood will be replaced by the mere "administration of things"—then what Hegel calls the Ethical Life (*Sittlichkeit*) of the State would no longer exist. There would be no need for patriotism, no calls for virtuous activity in service to the fatherland. Even the ethical ties of the family itself would begin to dissolve, as more and more people resort to the basic animality of selfish pursuits.

From a properly Hegelian perspective, what Kojève fails to see is that a state of affairs ruled by the mere "administration of things" would quickly undermine itself. Without at least some degree of *Sittlichkeit* to pull individuals out of themselves and their own selfish pursuits, no common goals can be pursued or accomplished.[2] As Hegel comments, "It is a grave miscalculation if the state, when it requires this sacrifice, is simply equated with civil society, and if its ultimate end is seen merely as *the security of the life and property* of individuals. For this security cannot be achieved by the sacrifice of what is supposed to be secured. . . . The ethical *moment of war* is implicit in what was stated above."[3] It is important to stress that Hegel is not here celebrating war. War is not always some great collective cause that unites a nation and preserves the health of the State. On the contrary, war truly is, for Hegel, a horrible affair in which the transience of our possessions and life itself becomes palpably real. It is therefore not something to be praised. However, *war is necessary* according to Hegel, for at the very least it can pull individuals out of their selfish pursuits and remind them that they are not the basis and ground of their own existence, that *they live within a greater whole* that encompasses them. This realization would not be possible at the End of History in a universal and homogeneous State. Here, individuals could carelessly pursue their own selfish ends without ever being reminded of the substantial basis of their existence.

But even the "mere administration of things" requires some individuals to dedicate themselves to the good of the whole. How would this dedication be possible if everyone were habituated exclusively to selfishness? Would we have to have two groups of people, those who work for the sake of the State and those who benefit from the State? But then how would one convince those working for the greater whole that their sacrifice is worth it, that while they are working as bureaucrats with the State's ends in mind, others are reaping the benefits of their labor? Why wouldn't they themselves simply act selfishly? Kojève's interpretation of Hegel on this point is at best misleading and at worst a deliberate falsification for ulterior motives. A universal and homogeneous global empire is neither possible nor desirable, since it would destroy its very basis in the spirit of a nation.

One of the consequences of Hegel's views on the necessity of multiple nations coexisting side by side, whether peacefully or violently, is that the *historical dialectic is bound to continue*. Nations, as Hegel states, always exist as *particular* manifestations of Spirit, and as such are *limited* by various shortcomings, idiosyncrasies, and contingent circumstances. As particular entities, States will always engage in relations with other States from a *particular standpoint* and perspective that includes the passions, vices, virtues, interests, ends, and talents of their population and rulers. Hegel highlights the implications of this observation:

In this turmoil, the ethical whole itself—the independence of the State—is *exposed to contingency*. The principles of the spirits of nations are in general of a limited nature because of that particularity in which they have their objective actuality and self-consciousness as existent individuals, and their deeds and destinies in their mutual relations are the manifest dialectic of the finitude of these spirits. It is through this dialectic that the universal spirit, the spirit of the world, produces itself in its freedom from all limits, and it is this spirit which exercises its right—which is the highest right of all—over finite spirits in world history as the *world's court of judgment*.[4]

This passage contains a fundamental ambiguity that is at the heart of the conflict of Hegelian hermeneutics. In one reading, Hegel is saying that History *is and always will be* a dialectic of finite spirits through which the most spiritually sensitive individuals—such as artists, the religious, and the philosophers—will be able to glimpse the infinite, universal spirit. As these spiritually sensitive individuals observe the course of historical events, they are simultaneously aware of their own *finitude* as persons living in a particular nation at a particular time and aware of their *infinitude* as persons able to *recognize* their own limitations. History, in this reading, is the final arbiter in the ideological disputes between nations. Yet this reading does not suggest that at some point in the historical dialectic, a single nation will come along that gets political order correct and thereby ends the dialectic. On the contrary, this reading suggests that each nation *participates* in truth and reason, but will ultimately fall into decay and die, since no single nation encompasses truth and reason. Nations, as Hegel never tires of repeating, are *particular individuals*, and as such have *negativity* as a component of their existence.

Another possible reading of the passage above—one more in line with Kojève's own—would argue that Hegel means to say that eventually the historical dialectic will end, since the Universal World Spirit produces itself from the historical dialectic. Those who take this view might also point to those passages in the section on World Spirit where Hegel appears to state explicitly that the historical dialectic's goal is to comprehend itself, something that Hegel's work has presumably accomplished.[5]

Yet this reading is flawed in several ways. First, based upon a close reading of the same passages used to support it, Hegel seems to suggest that Spirit's comprehension of itself—again, presumably carried out in his own work—functions as a *transition* to a higher stage of Spirit, one that he himself cannot comprehend or imagine. He states:

This comprehension is its being and principle, and the completion of an act of comprehension *is at the same time its alienation and transition*. To put it in formal terms, the spirit which comprehends this comprehension anew and which—and this amounts to the same thing—returns into itself from its alienation, is the spirit at a stage higher than that at which it stood in its earlier comprehension.[6]

Spirit does not just understand itself once and for all time. History shows us multiple efforts to understand Being, and Hegel's is simply the best, most complete, and most recent—at least, thus far. This passage seems to suggest that his act of comprehension will lead to a *transition* in the dialectic of Spirit, but definitely *not its end*. Many recent Hegel scholars confirm this reading.[7] Though he knows his act of comprehension will affect the historical course, he never mentions—because, most likely, he does not know—exactly how history will play itself out after he has made his mark. Hegel himself is one of those "unconscious instruments and organs of that inner activity in which the shapes which they themselves assume pass away, while the spirit in and for itself prepares and works its way towards the transition to its next and higher stage."[8] The future is unknown for Hegel. Although he claims to have comprehended the past, nowhere in his corpus—with the exception of a brief comment in the *Lectures on the Philosophy of World History* where he states that the future most likely lies with the United States and Russia—does he claim to forecast the future. "The owl of Minerva only flies at dusk," Hegel famously declared. It would be foolishness, from the Hegelian perspective, to attempt to predict how the historical course will play itself out.

Slavoj Zizek's recent publication fully substantiates this argument. Despite being tinged with his own political and social agenda, Zizek's book serves as a refreshingly novel attack on the "traditional" reading of Hegel that sees his work as a "swallowing" of all that is to be known by the Absolute. Zizek argues for a more modest Hegel, even going so far as to say that Hegel's great insight is that *neither the past nor the future* can be known "objectively." In this reading, the past and future always exist as *possibilities that are rearranged* depending upon events that occur in the present. There is a rather paradoxical link between the completeness of the past and our capacity to change it *retroactively*. Just as every great new work of art radically changes how one interprets the entire history of art, or every political revolution radically changes how one understands previous history, the past is never something that can be viewed from an impartial standpoint.[9] What Hegel seems to do in his "system," then, is to simply illustrate this principle from his current historical standpoint. He is fully aware of how he is *changing the past* in recapitulating it.

This principle applies even more to Hegel's stance on the future. Zizek appears to believe that Hegel pleads an almost radical ignorance on the future course of history, disclaiming all knowledge about where it could possibly be going. To quote him at length:

The question, however, remains: does Hegel's thought harbor such an openness towards the future, or does the closure of his system a priori preclude it?
In spite of misleading appearances, we should answer yes, Hegel's thought is
open towards the future, but precisely on account of its closure. That is to say,
Hegel's opening towards the future is a negative: it is articulated in his nega-
tive/limiting statements like the famous "one cannot jump ahead of one's time"
from his Philosophy of Right. The impossibility of directly borrowing from the
future is grounded in the very fact of retroactivity which makes the future a
priori unpredictable: we cannot climb onto our own shoulders and see ourselves
"objectively," in terms of the way we fit into the texture of history, because this
texture is again and again retroactively rearranged.[10]

Zizek interprets Hegel's claim that nations, cultures, and the individuals
living in them must necessarily exist "as particulars" in the following way:
because we constantly reinterpret the past based upon present historical
circumstances, human actors in history can never see themselves "as they
are" apart from their much skewed, particular perspective. Even Hegel,
according to Zizek, does not exempt himself from this insight. Hegel is very
much aware that his *Philosophy of History* is only a retrospective construction based upon his present historical perspective. Therein lies the closure of
Hegel's "system": it completely precludes the possibility of objective historical narratives and knowledge of the future. *It is complete insofar as it has
fully articulated this limitation.*

The notion of the "End of History" thus takes on a radically altered meaning for Zizek's Hegel. Far from meaning the final culminating point in the
historical dialectic, after which nothing of historical significance occurs, it
rather suggests Hegel's introduction of *self-relativization* into his system.
There is an irreducible gap between the various perspectives on the world—
between rich and poor, American and Chinese, male and female—but all
of these perspectives necessarily place themselves at the end of a historical
narrative. The End of History can apply to all of them. It is relativized and
historicized, since there exists no external measure by which to adjudicate
between conflicting perspectives. Here is Zizek again:

> Read in this way, the infamous "closure of the Hegelian system" is strictly cor-
> relative to its thorough (self-)relativization: the "closure" of the system does not
> mean that there is nothing outside the system (the naïve notion of Hegel as the
> individual who claimed to have achieved "Absolute knowledge of everything");
> it means that we are forever unable to "reflexivize" this Outside, to inscribe
> it within the Inside, even in the purely negative (and deceptively modest,
> self-deprecating) mode of acknowledging that reality is an absolute Otherness
> which forever eludes our grasp.[11]

Zizek here radicalizes certain tendencies he sees in Hegel. His position functions as the *inverse* of the Kojèvian one, taking just about every one of the latter's points of emphasis and saying that Hegel in fact meant the opposite. Alluding to it as the "traditional" reading of Hegel, Zizek gives Kojève's famous commentary in his *Introduction* a proper thrashing, leaving little leftover for contemporary End of History theorists. Yet as is commonly the case with reactionary interpretations, Zizek's own perhaps goes too far in the other direction. He provides a very thorough and coherent reading of Hegel based upon select passages from the latter's work. But it is difficult, when all is said and done, to accept it completely. While Kojève emphasizes those passages where Hegel claims "Absolute Knowledge" and Reason's victory in History—to the complete neglect of those passages showing more modesty and disclaiming all knowledge of the future—Zizek appears to do the opposite, focusing exclusively on those passages where Hegel pleads ignorance or relativizes himself.

Is some sort of compromise between these opposite interpretations possible? Is the true Hegel perhaps a bit more moderate, somewhere in between the Kojèvian *Sage* on the one hand and Zizek's unknowing radical on the other? Eric Michael Dale, while very sympathetic to Zizek's understanding of Hegel, argues for a much tamer version of him. In his view, Zizek's "tragic" vision of the Hegelian social process—where there is no hidden teleology guiding us and every intervention into history is a jump into the unknown—forgets about the weight of the past for the historical present and future. It may very well be true that human beings can never know the past "objectively." However, it is still the case that this past contains *limited possibilities* within it, that it determines which possibilities individuals and nations can actualize based upon their cultural, genetic, political, and religious inheritance. It is impossible that the future is complete openness and indeterminateness, since it is inextricably linked to a past, even if this past cannot be completely penetrated theoretically. As Dale comments, "Despite his talk of 'crushed potentials,' Zizekian historical freedom seems too Sartrean somehow, too 'free,' too cut loose from the historical or evental moorings which enable it to be what it is in the first place."[12] As correct as Zizek may be in his assertion that human beings cannot know the past or future, human action does not take place extended over an abyss of possibility.[13] Whether individuals are conscious of it or not, we all inherit certain possibilities from our past, which in turn determine the possible trajectories of the future. There is never pure openness before us, but a set of possibilities that our past history has determined beforehand. But we cannot know this history completely. This amounts to the insight that we never quite appreciate the potential lying within us on an individual and societal level.

Dale therefore finds it important to distinguish between two different understandings of historical progress: immanent and transcendent. Hegel, he argues, is first and foremost the philosopher of *immanent* historical progress, which means, to put it simply, that history is a process internal to itself. Spirit in history emerges "not as the game-master who moves pieces on the board, but as the motion of the pieces themselves as they *fulfill the role that they have as pieces on the board*."[14] A transcendent view of history would say the opposite, that there is some puppet master guiding the historical process—whether God, a telos, or transcendent Spirit. Zizek is correct in pointing out that to read Hegel's account of history as if he were advocating a transcendent view of historical progress would be both incorrect and dangerous. Yet he errs in believing that the removal of a transcendent historical *telos* means the future is radically open and unknowable. The immanent movements of the historical process—driven forward by concrete historical actors—still operate by means of what Lonergan would call "emergent probability." There are possibilities buried deep in the past and present that might or might not be actualized. These possibilities, while not determining the future, at least *limit the scope* of its possible course.

Interpreters who see an End of History in Hegel's work take what Dale calls a "top-down" view of history, in which a transcendent Idea manifests itself throughout the course of human history. But this take reads Hegel as more of a Platonist than an Aristotelian. Dale and Zizek agree that, for Hegel, there is no preordained universal plan made concrete within human life. Though sometimes Hegel's language and images play into this reading, it would be contrary to his explicit theoretical stance.[15] For Hegel, one must first of all take into account the concrete contingent facts of history before one can ever discern in it any sort of plan. It is only by means of these contingent facts that history moves forward. The historical process is immanent insofar as it works itself out according to the potentialities and possibilities inherent in human beings and the spirit they manifest. In order to know these potentialities and possibilities, one must closely study the raw facts of history and anthropology.

Dale argues that *Das Ende*, for Hegel, must be understood more in the sense of *culmination rather than finality*. As I mentioned earlier, the goal is first of all to grasp the conditions for the possibility of rational existence and flourishing. These conditions will provide a general standard for assessing historical developments. There is really no "particular end" in sight, other than this one, when it comes to historical analysis, due to the immanent nature of the historical dialectic. A result of this culmination is that philosophy can only pronounce upon events that have already occurred. Hegel repeatedly warns his readers about this limitation. The only thing Hegel does know with certainty is that Spirit will *somehow* manifest itself. The means whereby, and the manner in which, it does this are unknown. Hegel can only tell us how Spirit has manifested itself *thus far*. Quoting Daniel Berthold-Bond's *Hegel's Grand Synthesis: a Study of Being, Thought, and History,* Dale comments:

> The owl of wisdom takes its flight not at the end of history (what could that even mean?) but when all perceptions of history have been exhausted—this is why the light has grown dim, and the dusk metaphor is an apt one. "When Hegel speaks of the 'consummation' or 'completion' or 'coming to an end' or 'reaching the goal' of spirit . . . such pronouncements should be read as the fulfillment of the *telos* of a historical epoch, not of history or knowledge entire—a fulfillment which will give place to a new epoch, a new production and work of spirit" (Berthold-Bond 1989: 139). Many forms of life must grow old and die, as new ones spring to life; the owl of Minerva must launch into many flights, ere the pageant of history reaches whatever consummation does or does not await it: ecological collapse, the return of Christ, nuclear holocaust, the Omega Point, cosmic heat-death, the Big Bounce, technological singularity, more of the same, or any other mythic, cultural, technological, or scientific scenario one wants to entertain.[16]

After Hegel, history will continue, but on a different basis and ground than it had previously.

NOTES

1. Georg W. F. Hegel, *Elements of the Philosophy of Right*, ed. Allen Wood, tr. H. B. Nisbet (New York: Cambridge University Press, 1991), 362.

2. Hegel even goes so far as to say that if it were somehow possible to create a league of all nations or a universal State, then it would be necessary to "generate opposition and create an enemy." This fake enemy would presumably instill enough fear into the minds of the citizens of this universal state that they would feel it necessary to work for the good of the whole. See Ibid., 362.

3. Ibid., 361.

4. Ibid., 371.

5. See Ibid., 372.

6. Ibid. My emphasis.

7. For instance, see, Philip T. Grier, "The End of History and the Return of History," in *The Hegel Myths and Legends*, ed. Jon Stewart (Evanston: Northwestern University Press, 1996), 192.

8. Hegel, *Philosophy of Right*, 373.

9. Slavoj Zizek, *Less Than Nothing: Hegel and the Shadow of Dialectical Materialism* (New York: Verso Books, 2012), 209.

10. Ibid., 221.

11. Ibid., 392.

12. Eric Michael Dale, *Hegel, the End of History, and the Future* (Cambridge: Cambridge University Press, 2014), 212.

13. An interesting comparison here would take account of Bernard Lonergan's theory of "emergent probability," which basically amounts to an analysis of statistical laws and how they make possible "schemes of recurrence" given certain scenarios. See the chapter on "Common Sense as Object" in Lonergan's *Insight* (Toronto: University of Toronto Press, 1992), 232.

14. Dale, *Hegel, the End of History, and the Future*, 17.

15. Ibid., 4.

16. Ibid., 220.

Chapter 22

What Is Hegel's Position on the End of History?

In clarifying Eric Voegelin's position on Historiogenesis in the second part of this study, I made a crucial distinction that will be extremely helpful for comprehending the undeniable ambiguity of the Hegelian position on the End of History. There, I distinguished between "tradition-bound" history—a history written within the theoretical and cultural matrix of a tradition, and limited by certain presuppositions about world-order—and "genuinely universal" history, which Voegelin calls a "mystery in the process of revelation." The former is the history in which we all live and conduct our everyday lives. It is also the history historians write, since nobody can step outside of their limited historical epoch to contemplate history as a whole. The latter, thus, is and will remain a mystery to human beings, as it is the history into which limited societies, cultures, and traditions enter when they are created, and the history out of which they will pass when these same societies, cultures, and traditions die or transform.

As we have seen, interpreters of Hegel fall into one of two possible camps. There are, first, those who emphasize and interpret Hegel's entire system in light of those passages where Hegel stresses the finality of his system and the end of history, art, religion, and philosophy—what Zizek calls the "traditional reading" of Hegel. Kojève, Fukuyama, and Popper, among others, fall into this camp. Second, there are those who, like Dale, Drury, and Zizek himself, emphasize those passages where Hegel very explicitly leaves his system open to revision and recognizes history as open to a mysterious future with unpredictable possibilities. All of these interpreters commit the same mistake: they highlight those passages that fit with their own understanding of the Hegelian position, and they either minimize or dismiss entirely those that contradict it. They operate with strict dualisms here. Hegel either leaves history open to a mysterious future or he does not; Hegel either acknowledges that his system could be overcome in the future or he does not; Hegel either overcomes art and religion in his system or he does not; and so on. But are these "either/or" interpretations necessary? Furthermore, would they even be true to the nature of Hegelian dialectics, which, by affirming *contradiction* and *tension* as the motor force of theoretical progress, overcomes all rigid dualisms?

I would make the case that Hegel *deliberately* leaves these holes or gaps in his work, if for no other reason than to show that they are *inherent to the structure of reality*. What is more, I believe it is possible to render these gaps intelligible by applying the key distinction mentioned above to Hegel's conflicting statements about the End of History. Though he had not formulated the vocabulary to synthesize these conflicts, Hegel was aware of the fact that there are *two types of history*. Hegel did indeed claim to bring history to an end, as Kojève argues. But which history? It is the history of a very limited epoch marked by certain presuppositions about metaphysics, ontology, and human nature. Within the theoretical framework of this historical epoch—that is, as a tradition-bound historian—Hegel can indeed claim that he has brought history to an end. When he alleges that philosophy has been completed in his system, he possibly means philosophy *as it has been understood by his historical epoch*. The problem with Kojève's interpretation of Hegel is that he understands Hegel's statements about finality as if they were being applied to Universal History. This mistake opens up the possibility for the radical interpretive distortions one sees in Kojève's work. He forgets that Hegel also explicitly *disclaimed all knowledge* of the future course of history, and in fact knew that neither he nor any other philosopher or historian could ever bring history to a close. But, again, which history? I would argue that Hegel pleads ignorance as to the future course of genuinely "Universal History." Like Voegelin, Hegel believes Universal History is a "mystery in the process of revelation."

Hegel's own words substantiate this interpretation. In a frequently cited passage from his *Philosophy of History*, Hegel claims that while the Europe of his day is growing old and dying, since the ground and basis of its history has worked itself out, America represents the land of the future. Hegel comments:

> Napoleon is reported to have said: "Cette vieille Europe m'ennuie." It is for America to abandon the ground on which hitherto the history of the world has developed itself. What has taken place in the New World up to the present time is only an echo of the Old World—the expression of a foreign life; and as a land of the future, it has no interest for us here, for as regards history, our concern must be with that which has been and that which is.[1]

Hegel very clearly distinguishes between *two different historical epochs* in this passage. The ground on which Europe's history has played itself out—complete with the economic, political, spiritual, and artistic complements to it—is weary and worn, and Hegel's philosophy is simply the Owl of Minerva taking its flight at dusk in Europe's day. Yet World History and World Spirit are not coextensive with European History and European Spirit. Hegel is very much aware that genuinely universal history transcends and moves beyond his own tradition-bound historiography. Whatever the new ground of history ends up being—maybe a new dominant religious tradition, the scientific method, or a raw power struggle—it cannot be and will not be the ground that formed the basis of Hegel's own thought. For, as Hegel claimed, "each individual is in any case a child of his time; thus philosophy too is its own time comprehended in thought. It is just as foolish to imagine that any philosophy can transcend its contemporary world as that an individual can overleap his own time or leap over Rhodes."[2] Hegel's philosophy is *his own time*—his own historical epoch—comprehended in thought, nothing more.[3]

As Grier, Dale, and Zizek have suggested in their work on Hegel, one might argue that Hegel's thought *is final for the very same reason that it is provisional.* He is the first philosopher to introduce *self-relativity* into his own system. Though it may seem paradoxical—Hegel, of course, demonstrated that many apparent paradoxes were not paradoxes at all—there is a sense in which each and every historical epoch could have its own philosopher who completes it. This pronouncement could then, in turn, be viewed as having been provisional by the succeeding age.[4] This insight brings me to my major thesis: *what is not provisional is Hegel's statement that all philosophies are provisional.* Because every philosopher—indeed, every human being—is bound by the theoretical and practical limitations of their historical epoch, it is impossible for anybody to gaze upon the entirety of history and take it in as a whole. However, certain men are born and live in special times—when a historical epoch has grown old and weary, and is about to die—and are thus perfectly situated to make sense of the historical course as it has developed into their present time. These men bring *a historical epoch* to an end, but not universal history.

The Voegelinian and Hegelian positions on the End of History are not, after all, that much different. Voegelin vociferously attacks Hegel for apparently attempting to provide himself with some sort of certainty about the future course of history. But as we have seen, this was a Hegel largely interpreted through the lens of Kojève's "code." The true Hegel would agree with Voegelin that no philosopher—no matter how intelligent, observant, and wise—can stand on his own shoulders to predict the future course of history. While Voegelin's criticisms of the "stop-history" movements carry great weight and can help us to understand the existential and theoretical intricacies of gnostic theorists, one cannot responsibly apply them to Hegel. The latter's thought is much more complex and self-aware than Voegelin gives it credit for and in fact allows for a much broader view of philosophy and history than is at first apparent. Kojève, not Hegel, paints an imaginary Second Reality that gives him existential closure. Kojève, not Hegel, attempted to achieve certainty about the future course of civilization. Kojève, not Hegel, thought that history had come to an end. Kojève, not Hegel, believed that philosophy, religion, and art, the highest pursuits of the human spirit, were now outdated and finished.[5] Kojève, as interesting and thought provoking as his work may be, should not be used as the interpretive "code" for understanding Hegel.

NOTES

1. Georg W. F. Hegel, *Lectures on the Philosophy of History*, tr. J. Sibree (New York: Dover Publications, 1956), 87.

2. Georg W. F. Hegel, *Elements of the Philosophy of Right*, ed. Allen Wood, tr. H. B. Nisbet (New York: Cambridge University Press, 1991), 21–22.

3. The obvious counterpoint to this assertion would of course be Hegel's own statement in the Introduction to his *Science of Logic* that his philosophy is "truth as it is without veil and as it is in its absolute nature. It can therefore be said that this content is the exposition of God as he is in his eternal being before the creation of nature and a finite mind." *Science of Logic* (tr. A. V. Miller [Amherst: Humanity Books, 1969], 50). One of the major problems with this objection is that it fails to take account of Hegel's own warnings against taking this part of his thought in abstraction from the other parts. Also, as the *Science of Logic* in many ways exposes the nature of the historical dialectic, the eternal aspect of his system may be more of an account of how his system will eventually be overcome, something in line with Bernard Lonergan's statement that everything can be revised except for the possibility of revision.

4. Phillip Grier, "The End of History and the Return of History," in *The Hegel Myths and Legends*, Jon Stewart (Evanston: Northwestern University Press, 1996), 192.

5. Indeed, it is precisely the finitude of each nation that, for Hegel, opens it up for the possibility of transcendence in Art, Religion, and Philosophy.

Chapter 23

Hegel on Transcendence and the "Beyond"

The primary thesis of this book is that Voegelin has misunderstood Hegel on the question of the End of History. Yet in arguing for this thesis, it seems I have broached many related topics of equal theoretical importance, not the least of which has been the question of transcendence and the "beyond." In the first chapter, I highlighted one of Voegelin's major contributions to a coherent philosophical anthropology—namely, the assertion that the human experience of transcendence is fundamental, and any theory that overlooks or underemphasizes this fact will be defective. One issue I have not yet addressed is Voegelin's accusation that Hegel seeks to eliminate the transcendent pole of human existence by absorbing divinity into himself. In this final chapter, I will attempt to address briefly this very issue.

The first thing that should be mentioned is that Thomas Altizer's provocative statement that Voegelin's attack on Hegel amounts to an Oedipal attack on his own father is not all that far from the truth. Voegelin, whether consciously or not, has appropriated numerous theoretical elements from Hegel's own thought, and while the tone and language he uses to describe these aspects of reality may differ considerably from Hegel's, the similarities must be acknowledged.[1] One of the most important is their focus on the "polar" dimensions of human reality and consciousness. Here, Voegelin and Hegel agree on fundamentals. To quote from Hegel's 1827 *Lectures on the Philosophy of Religion*:

> When human beings think of God, they elevate themselves above the sensible, the external, the singular. We say that it is an elevation to the pure, to that which is at one with itself. This elevation is a transcending of the sensible, of mere feeling, a journey into the pure region; and this region of the universal is thought. . . . It is also not an inert, abstract universal, however, but rather the absolute womb or the infinite fountainhead out of which everything emerges,

163

into which everything returns, and in which it is *eternally maintained.* This basic determination is therefore the definition of God as substance.[2]

Like Voegelin, Hegel situates the human being between two "poles," that of the concrete, finite, and particular, and that of the universal and divine. The human essence is to live in the tension this dual polarity creates. What makes human beings unique, for Hegel, is *universalizing thought*, which allows them to abstract completely from all determinate particulars in the concrete world around them. But they still have to live in a world of finite particulars—their own bodily concreteness with hunger, thirst, and digestion. Our ability to abstract from this particular concreteness allows us, in a sense, to recognize that there is in fact a "beyond" to all of the particular finite things we see in front of us. God, as he exists in his universal inner being, cannot be identified with any particular object of the external world. He is "Beyond" all of them.

Hegel allows for at least some form of transcendence and an appreciation of the "Beyond" of the finite world. God, as the absolute fountainhead and concrete ground of everything finite in the universe, does indeed exist and transcends both the bodily-located human being and the finite world around him. Additionally, as in Voegelin's analysis of Thing-reality and It-reality, there is a *necessary relation* between these two poles: the universal and all-encompassing entails the particular and finite just as much as the particular and finite entails the universal and all-encompassing. These are the two poles that human consciousness mediates and *must* mediate. For this reason, Hegel warns us against both pantheism—which completely identifies God with concrete particular objects—and a sort of religion that would see the divine as so transcending the world that He has nothing at all to do with it or can exist in some abstraction apart from it. Both these religious representations are products of what Hegel calls the abstract understanding (*Verstand*).

Hegel has even more to say about the "beyond" and its relationship to the finite world. I quote him at length:

The infinite is just infinite, and we are finite, for our knowledge, feeling, reason, and spirit are limited and persist in their limitedness. But this talk is already contradicted in what has been said. *It is undoubtedly correct that we are limited;* so we are not talking about the limitedness of nature but about the dependence of reason. However, it is equally correct that this finite element has no truth, *and reason is precisely the insight that the finite is only a limit.* But inasmuch as we know something as a limit, *we are already beyond it.* The animal or the stone knows nothing of its limit. In contrast, the I, as knowing or thinking in general, is limited but knows about the limit, and in this very knowledge the limit is only limit, only something negative outside us, and I am beyond it . . . we must not have such absurd respect in the presence of the infinite. The infinite is the wholly pure abstraction, the initial abstraction of being according to which limit is omitted—a being that relates itself to itself, the universal within which every boundary is ideal, is sublated. Therefore, the finite does not endure, and inasmuch as it does not endure, there is also no longer a gulf present between finite and infinite, they are no longer two.[3]

Hegel would thus say that our acknowledgment of a "beyond" of finite things, to which our minds lack access, is one of the paradoxes at the heart of human existence. Unlike a rock, a plant, or a dog, we as humans know that we are limited, that our existence is in the realm of the finite and particular, and that we can never truly escape it. Yet this is precisely what establishes our relationship to the infinite beyond. The infinite and the beyond become, in a sense, *incarnate* in the human psyche as an established necessary connection between the two poles. There is an "identity-in-difference" between the here-and-now and the beyond, as well as between the finite and the infinite. There *is* a "beyond" for Hegel. Reason is essentially this "beyond" insofar as it stands in an infinite relationship both to itself and the divine ground of reality.

As I mentioned, Hegel seems to suggest that human experience consists of two different poles, "God and the consciousness for which God is."[4] These two poles share an essential and inseparable relation to each other. Finite human beings, though distinct from the divine, can "raise" their consciousness to it through a process of transcendence. Likewise, the divine "lowers" itself to the human by realizing itself in consciousness. Human consciousness, for Hegel, seems to be the center in which these two poles meet and mediate each other. Whereas Kant faults human Understanding (*Verstand*) for giving rise to various antinomies, and thus places the "Beyond" in a "*Ding-an-sich*," a thing in itself, Hegel asserts a direct mirroring between our consciousness of reality and reality as it is in itself. For Hegel, the antinomies are not simply due to the limitation of human consciousness but are actually part of the structure of reality itself:

> If our conception of the world is dissolved by the transference to it of the determinations of the infinite and the finite, *still more is spirit itself, which contains both of them, inwardly self-contradictory and self-dissolving*: it is not the nature of the material or the object to which they are applied or in which they occur that can make a difference, for it is only through those determinations and in accordance with them that the objects contain the contradiction.[5]

Reality, all of God's creation, is in a sense antinomic, and the two poles of human consciousness mediate one another in this paradoxical way. Hegel's analysis here is similar to Voegelin's articulation of the paradox inherent in the complex "consciousness-reality-language." The paradox, for the latter,

plays itself out in our consciousness, in the reality in which our consciousness participates, and in the language we use to express our awareness of this
participation.

Yet one may object here, as Voegelin does, that Hegel obfuscates the
language he uses to describe the relationship between these two poles just
enough to suggest that human beings can be *identified with* the divine, and
that nothing in the divine remains outside the scope of human intelligence.
What, for instance, is the *Science of Logic* if not Hegel's self-identification
with God's thoughts before creation?[6] Does this necessarily entail a complete
absorption of the divine thought? Can the Godhead still have "thoughts" with
which we, or Hegel, cannot identify? Or does Hegel claim to exhaust the
divine thought with his own?

According to Hegel,

> *God and I are distinct from one another.* If both were one, then there would be
> an immediate self-relation, one without mediation and without relation, i.e., a
> unity without distinction. In that the two are distinct, *each one is not what the
> other is.* But if they are nevertheless connected, or have identity at the same
> time as their distinctiveness, then this identity itself is distinct from their distinct
> being; it is something different from both of them because otherwise they would
> not be distinct.[7]

When Hegel talks about the "inner unity of the divine and human," he
does not at all mean that Human Beings are living Gods or that he himself is
God. Rather, one must keep in mind his insistence on Reason as Identity-in-
Difference. Human beings have an *aspect* of their nature that can be identified
with the divine, while at the same time remaining different or distinct from
it. All human beings participate in the divine; the divine participates in every
human being. This claim is Hegel's reflection on the Judeo-Christian notion
that man is made "in the image and likeness of God."

Of God as He is in Himself, as the eternally complete object of our transcending rational activity, Hegel does attempt to speak conceptually:

> Only when grasped as concrete is it Spirit; but even in its determination as inter-
> nally concrete *it remains this unity with itself,* this one actuality that we have just
> now denominated as substance. . . . [S]o if we speak of a beginning, we have
> this one actuality as a relating of itself to itself and not to another; we do not yet
> have an advance, a concrete being . . . (yet) *all through the development God
> does not step outside this unity with himself.*[8]

God, always advancing toward the human intellectual penetration of Him, also
remains in a unity with Himself in his eternal essence. This eternal essence,
this "unity with himself," is the object of Rational thought, according to

Hegel in the *Science of Logic*. This passage gets at the fundamental difference between Voegelin and Hegel: while both affirm the paradox in the complex of "consciousness-reality-language," the former insists that there is a "beyond" of this complex, that this paradoxical complex *does not exhaust* the entirety of Being. Voegelin would suggest that there are two aspects to the divine ground: one that can be comprehended by the human intellect and another that remains *outside of* the human intellectual horizon, eternally complete in itself apart from creation. Therefore, even if we cannot know God as He is in Himself, we can know Him *as He is in relationship to us*. Voegelin calls this the *"Parousia* of the Beyond." The divine ground of existence is real to us as the presence of a beyond and the beyond of this presence. This is a key difference between Hegel and Voegelin. Hegel claims to have solved every mystery about the divine. He claims to have articulated the divine essence as it stands in relation to us, precisely as thought or Logic, the universal pole of our consciousness, and *this relation is all there is*. For Hegel, there is no "beyond" to this relationship.

The passages above seem to suggest that Voegelin and Hegel have very similar views on the paradoxic structure of human consciousness, the fact that this paradoxic consciousness is a mirror of the paradoxic structure of reality, and also that our language, for this same reason, is also paradoxic. Unlike Kant, who claims that the paradoxes of reality (antinomies) are the result of the limitations in our own Understanding, Voegelin and Hegel allege that reality itself is paradoxical and antinomical. Does this mean, however, that both think the transcendent God as he is in himself is paradoxical? Voegelin would probably plead ignorance on this question. For him, the mystery of this Beyond remains part of the structure of reality. Hegel, on the other hand, would say that the Godhead itself is paradoxical, "eternally complete and eternally completing itself." It must be acknowledged that there is indeed something like transcendence in Hegel's thought, but it does not quite do justice to the radicalness of the "beyond" to which Voegelin directs our attention. There is the "raising of the heart and mind to the eternal and all-encompassing ground of our existence," but this ground, for Hegel, can be intellectually penetrated. Voegelin, on the other hand, believes part of the divine mind can be discerned while another part is always beyond our finitude. Thus, after all, Voegelin's accusation in *In Search of Order* that Hegel turns the mystery of It-reality into concepts upon which speculation in Thing-reality is possible may prove true. Instead of using the language of participation, Hegel uses the language of "reflective identity."[9]

To state it again, what precisely separates Voegelin and Hegel on the topic of the "beyond"? Hegel does not truly get beyond the mystery of the beyond, according to Voegelin. He simply obfuscates the distinctions in the complex of consciousness-reality-language, claiming that the mystery of the Divine

Beyond as it has to do with reality has been penetrated, when in reality all he has done is to bring this mystery into his philosophical language. Voegelin keeps all elements of the complex consciousness-reality-language in their proper places, and also claims that it is part of the structure of reality that there is both an aspect of the "beyond" that makes itself present (*Parousia*) to our consciousness and an aspect of the beyond that transcends our consciousness. *But the fact of its transcending our consciousness is also present to our consciousness.* Hegel, as far as I can tell, never makes this crucial distinction. Voegelin, therefore, perhaps correctly accuses Hegel of immanentizing the It-reality, of making it incarnate in the human psyche without fully acknowledging that aspect of the beyond that is truly beyond our psyche's horizon.

NOTES

1. Also see Jürgen Gebhardt's Epilogue to Voegelinl's *In Search of Order*, where he acknowledges that "Voegelin's analysis of the reflective dimension of consciousness is informed by Hegel's attempt at recovering the experiential roots of consciousness. In opposition to, and as a corrective of, the symbolism of reflective identity, Voegelin says, he has formulated the symbolism of reflective distance. Following the lead of Hegel's self-analysis in the *Phaenomenologie des Geistes*, Voegelin reenacts by means of anamnesis the true story of the unfolding of reflective consciousness from its mythopoetic origins in Hesiod to its full differentiation in Plato-socrates" (133).

2. Georg W. F. Hegel, *Lectures on the Philosophy of Religion*, ed. Peter Hodgson, tr. R. F. Brown, P. C. Hodgson, and J. M. Stewart (New York: Oxford University Press, 2007), 122.

3. Ibid., 173.

4. Ibid., 129.

5. See Hegel's *Science of Logic*, tr. A. V. Miller (Amherst: Humanity Books, 1969), 47. My emphasis.

6. Ibid., 50.

7. Hegel, *Lectures on the Philosophy of Religion,* 164.

8. Ibid., 119.

9. Eric Voegelin, *In Search of Order* (Columbia: University of Missouri Press, [2000]), 63.

Conclusion

TRANSCENDENCE, DEATH, AND
THE SEARCH FOR ORDER

In the final, unfinished volume of *Order and History*, *In Search of Order*, Voegelin's approach to philosophizing became even more meditative than it had in any of the previous volumes. As a finite man staring down the imminent prospect of his own death, he struggled to find the words to articulate his concrete experience of transcendence. Hence, the existential dimension of his search for truth took on heightened significance. He became, in a word, *Eros* embodied.

It is curious, then, that at this critical point in his life, Voegelin would return yet again to reflect on Hegel. After the hyperbolic lashing of the 1972 "On Hegel: A Study in Sorcery" and the devastating critiques of *The Ecumenic Age* in 1974, Voegelin's tone in this final volume is noticeably more restrained. In fact, as had been the norm much earlier in his career, reserved praise seems to emanate from every line. It is almost as if Voegelin, in the final days of his life, wanted to meet up with his greatest intellectual companion one last time. While the usual criticisms are emphasized, they are presented more in the tone of the gripes and grievances of two intimate mates who had spent the majority of their lives together.

Both Voegelin and Hegel found themselves living in times of intense spiritual, intellectual, and societal disorder. Both struggled to extricate themselves from this disorder, and ultimately viewed the philosophic enterprise itself as part of the solution. Both needed to find a way out of the Cave of untruth into the light of truth. Voegelin, in fact, explicitly references this kinship with Hegel: "Hegel is in the position of the prisoner, openly in revolt against the shadows in the Cave of his age, be they doctrinal deformations of theology, propositional deformations of metaphysics or ontology, clever intellectualism, second-rate criticism or skepticism, ecstatically phantasizing exuberance, edifying sermonizing, or sentimental, thoughtless elevation. So far Hegel's movement is the same as the Platonic."[1] Because, as Voegelin would repeat, resistance to untruth is the origin of the search for truth, Hegel's philosophic quest was in some ways no different from Voegelin's own, and could justifiably be considered one of the greatest, in the same league as Plato's or St. Augustine's.

But as we noted in the last chapter of this study, there are a number of subtle differences in the ways these thinkers approached questions of transcendence that would ultimately have important implications for the societal consequences of their thought. Whereas Plato and Voegelin understood the prisoner in the Cave as having undergone a *Periagoge*—a "turning around" or "conversion," at least partially induced by the transcendent divine pole of existence—Hegel's revolt against the shadows of the Cave risks becoming a self-assertive act. Whereas Plato's and Voegelin's escape from the cave of untruth still entails existence in the *metaxy*—the in-between of the divine human tension—Hegel's language suggests the possibility of doing away with the tension altogether. The paradoxes manifest by the divine pole of existence are not an unresolvable mystery in the process of revelation, as they are for Voegelin, but have become part of the objective structure of reality itself. Perhaps this is the key to appreciating the real difference between these two great thinkers.

It is frightening to think that the world we inhabit today is in many respects similar to the ones Voegelin and Hegel confronted. Despite the unprecedented increases in wealth, health, and quality of life that we've witnessed since the end of World War II and, more especially, since the collapse of the Soviet Union, attentive thinkers cannot help but have a creeping sense of impending disaster, as if the entire scaffolding for the degree of order we have come to take for granted has been established on an abyss of nihilism. We fear that this omnipresent nihilism will soon bear fruit in the form of a murderous eschatological ideology. The signs are everywhere, from the increasing ethnonationalism of the far right to the sometimes violent and always resentful "woke" identity politics of the far left. In the midst of luxury and comfort, despair and anxiety seem to reign supreme. Yet, what is truly scary about these trends is not so much the fact of their existence but rather the fact that the traditional sources of remedying this existential nihilism are either under attack themselves or have been completely forgotten altogether. The greatest exemplars of the spiritual quest for truth and order, beauty and goodness, are a diminishing presence on the Western cultural scene, as education has become a mere means for economic "progress" or an experimentation lab for various cultural fads and ideologies. Less and less in America and in Western civilization more broadly are students exposed to Plato, Homer, St.

Augustine, Camus, or Shakespeare. Because we are swimming in a cultural milieu that truly believes history has come to, or will shortly come to, an end, raising the most basic of human questions and trying to learn from the wisdom of past quests for order are viewed as unnecessary at best, and dangerous to the ideological status quo at worst. If we ever want to restore some degree of order and stave off the extreme disorder to come, resurrecting this dialogue with the past is crucial. In this endeavor, we can learn a great deal from both Voegelin and Hegel. One day we might, in a reversal of Voegelin's first section of *In Search of Order* entitled "The Beginning of the Beginning," bring about the "End of the End."

NOTES

1. Eric Voegelin, *In Search of Order* (Columbia: University of Missouri Press, 2000), 71.

Appendix A

VOEGELIN, HEGEL, AND TWENTY-FIRST CENTURY ESCHATOLOGICAL IDENTITY POLITICS

As this study has attempted to address not only a key scholarly debate dealing with the relationship between three profound thinkers, but has also sought thereby to speak on theoretical issues currently playing themselves out in our contemporary political and cultural scene, it would be amiss not to offer a concluding statement that puts Hegel and Voegelin into "direct contact" with the contemporary world. We live in a world characterized fundamentally by stop-history movements. These movements permeate every corner of civil society, the State, and, increasingly, the family itself. In America specifically, we are currently experiencing a constitutional, moral, and economic crisis stemming from these influences. We may not know the ultimate consequences of this crisis for years to come. However, its key features are becoming increasingly clear. The following is thus a summative reflection on contemporary American politics as it has come to be marked by a unique blend of secularized eschatology and what Fukuyama calls "identity politics."

PLURALISM AND THE CHALLENGE OF COMMUNICATION

No doubt, American history has always had its fair share of political infighting, dysfunction, and raw instability. Those living through the traumas of the 1960s and early 1970s probably felt the world was crashing down, and democracy itself was on its last leg. In the Civil War, of course, American democracy truly was in peril, leaving in its wake hundreds of thousands of untold American deaths. But somehow, miraculously, one might say, it has always managed to resurrect itself phoenix-like from the ashes of its historical dustbin.[1] The possibility of communication between individuals and groups who disagree on fundamental issues remains the basis for this renewal. The conflicting interests and visions of reality held by these groups certainly make communication difficult and time-consuming. Rarely are they able to compromise, and rarer still form a consensus. Yet, while communication has always been a challenge in American democracy, never has the inability to communicate become a *fundamental principle* of a powerful coalition within either political party. Nevertheless, precisely this has happened in recent decades. The Alt-Right and certain factions of what has come to be known as the Anti-Racist movement on the Left hold this impossibility of communication to be axiomatic. According to some within these movements, by virtue of the fact that one is white, black, or Latino, a member of the LGBTQ+ community or a particular religious organization, one cannot help but participate in a culture with its own specific logic and worldview.[2] The transmission of ideas and evidence beyond the horizon of this worldview is futile. And so, politics becomes a matter of speaking one's "own truth," a unique reality in the vein of Rousseauian self-expression. This mode of thought is directly tied to the "identity politics" Fukuyama highlighted in his *End of History and the Last Man* and has its deep intellectual origins in Kojève's work as interpreted through the lens of postmodernism.

Of course, when it comes to the Anti-Racists, we should recall that criticizing overt racism or advocating for multiculturalism and diversity does not necessitate holding this extreme view. Eric Voegelin himself was a passionate advocate for some elements of the multiculturalist and antiracist positions.[3] His corpus demonstrates that we have a lot to learn from the various texts, traditions, and world peoples. It also reveals confidence in every human person's fundamental dignity, insofar as he or she is a possible locus of the divine "Parousia" in reality. In fact, Voegelin can offer us a much clearer vision of what a healthy, vibrant, and nondeological antiracism might look like and could help us to avoid its often too readily accepted derailments.[4]

On the other side, when it comes to the Alt-Right, we must acknowledge that passionate patriotism and the sense of identity it entails is not necessarily a damaging political force. Patriotism, as Hegel observes, inspires individuals to sacrifice and die for a greater good beyond themselves. However, Voegelin reminds us that an immoderate, unbalanced, and blind nationalism that fails to recognize its own faults or listen to contrary perspectives will lead inevitably to its own destruction. It is an ideology no less dangerous than the forces aiming to tear down the nation.

Political communication, according to Voegelin, is of two primary sorts: substantive and pragmatic.[5] Substantive communication entails an effort to build the individual's personality and thus create the conditions for the possibility of substantive order in the community. It focuses on authentic dialogue, spiritual edification, virtue, and moderate forms of civic responsibility. Much of what takes place in a healthy education system would fit into this category of communication. As a place where the youth can dialogue with differing perspectives, learn about their identities, what it means to be a human being, the virtues of moderation, temperance, compromise, and courage, as well as how they can individually be a source of order in the larger world, an educational institution that focuses on substantive communication would have no ulterior motive other than the growth and health (physical, spiritual, intellectual, and emotional) of its students.

On the other hand, pragmatic communication aims to induce people to behave in such a manner that their behavior will agree with the communicator's purpose, whether ideological or commercial. The plethora of political campaign advertisements we recently witnessed in the buildup to the 2020 presidential election is a case in point. Playing on the viewers' emotions like levers, these advertisements' goal was no less than to excite individuals to go through the effort of voting, even if the particular candidate for whom they voted did not truly represent their real interests. Psychological manipulation thus abounds in pragmatic communication and is its fundamental driving force.

Voegelin suggests that, in democracy, both substantial and pragmatic communication are essential, but their respective roles and the coordination between them is somewhat problematic. For instance, the extreme right has shown that it is sometimes difficult to distinguish rhetoric meant for encouraging civic virtue from an ideological manipulation that tries to incorporate people into a societal war-machine. On the other end of the spectrum, some left-wing movements have shown us that encouraging political activism and social justice, while purporting to build the budding activists' character, in reality aims to overthrow the perceived "oppressors" in a vengeful struggle for power. Both extremes of the political spectrum use pragmatic communication to advance ideological causes, resulting ultimately in the inevitable breakdown of substantial order. Few doubt this reality. Yet, pragmatic communication does have a role to play in promoting political health. Commercial advertisements can and do open up consumers to products and solutions that deal with real needs. Likewise, though walking a fine line between jingoism and civic virtue, patriotic propaganda can inspire individuals to serve a country in ways necessary for its healthy functioning.

The critical problem in the United States is that the fundamental difficulty of distinguishing between these two forms of communication risks being transformed into the postulate that there is no distinction at all. There is a widespread tendency to view *all* substantive communication as merely *veiled attempts* at pragmatic communication. In this view, the fundamental political and philosophic questions about which people disagree—How should I live my life? What are my obligations to country and individual? What are my rights in regard to this same country and these same individuals?—are off-limits to discussion, and, what is more, should not even be posed in the first place. This rejection of the "question" is precisely the temptation to which the extreme Right and the Anti-Racist movement have fully succumbed.

ANTI-RACISM, THE EXTREME RIGHT, AND THE ANATOMY OF IDEOLOGY

One of the best-selling books on racism in the last few years is entitled *White Fragility: Why White People Find It So Hard to Talk about Racism* by Robin DiAngelo. The basic thesis is that white people—even those who would consider themselves extremely progressive and "WOKE"—cannot help being racist since they are the products and unwitting perpetuators of "white privilege" or the "white collective." If a white person tries to defend himself or herself against the charge of racism—say, by pointing out the fact that they have black friends, colleagues, and acquaintances, and that race is not a factor in how they treat these individuals—they thereby engage in what DiAngelo calls "white fragility." Some of the most common behaviors associated with white fragility are physically leaving the room when confronted about one's racism, emotional withdrawal, arguing, denying, focusing on intentions rather than impact, and avoiding racially uncomfortable situations. Most important of all for the possibility of cross-racial communication, *she claims that the appeal to contrary evidence, or criticizing of her own argument, is itself proof that one is racist and is perhaps the most significant manifestation of white fragility.*

In cross-racial dynamics, race is *always* a factor, according to DiAngelo, if not for the white person, then certainly for the black person. In relating a personal anecdote, she illustrates this logic:

> I was co-leading a workshop with an African American man. A white participant said to him, "I don't see race; I don't see you as black." My co-trainer's response was, "Then how will you see racism?" He then explained to her that he was black, he was confident that she could see this, and that his race meant that he had a very different experience in life than she did. If she were ever going to understand or challenge racism, she would need to acknowledge this difference. Pretending that she did not notice that he was black was not helpful to him in any way, as it denied his reality—indeed, it refused his reality—and kept hers insular and unchallenged. This pretense that she did not notice his race assumed that he was "just like her," and in so doing, she projected her reality onto him.

For example, I feel welcome at work so you must too; I have never felt that my race mattered, so you must feel that yours doesn't either. But of course, we do see the race of other people, and race holds deep social meaning for us.[6]

Because the white participant in this passage has never had to face discrimination, she has the "privilege" *not to* see color when interacting with other human beings. In a twist of irony, her indifference to the color of someone's skin is in fact the greatest proof of her white privilege, which reinforces racial boundaries. As a white person herself, DiAngelo concludes that the best a white person can do is to acknowledge one's privilege and subconscious racism and, painstakingly throughout one's life, try to remedy it, though with the full awareness that it can never be fully overcome.

Notwithstanding their overwhelming popularity in American society today, DiAngelo's theories of "white privilege" and "white racism" have several dangerous consequences. First, one cannot help recalling Hannah Arendt's rejection of the declarations of collective guilt during the Holocaust war-crime tribunals: "When all are guilty, no one is; confessions of collective guilt are the best possible safeguard against the discovery of culprits."[7] If the terms "racist" and "white supremacist" apply equally to white progressives and Ku Klux Klan members; if one, despite overt acts of kindness, respect, and goodwill is lumped into the same groups of people who have performed lynchings, mob violence, and owned slaves, then we lose the ability as a society to make the moral and legal distinctions necessary to hold the latter groups of people truly accountable. Judgments become impossible, as all whites and all blacks dissolve into their respective "realities." Since "universalism" is an integral part of white culture and merely serves to perpetuate white privilege, alleges DiAngelo, no race can communicate with any other race on topics of right and wrong, accountability and responsibility. This attempt at communication would itself fall into the all-consuming vortex of racism and white privilege. "Guilt" would therefore not exist, as the entire concept requires a *shared* understanding of standards of behavior and crime.

Secondly, DiAngelo's analysis of race relations irresponsibly overlooks a wide range of historical phenomena that disprove her thesis that the black experience of repression and discrimination is unique and that whites are the only oppressive group.[8] In her analysis, she equates predicting this counterargument with actually refuting it. This obfuscation, for Eric Voegelin, is a sure sign of an ideological thinker.[9] There exists to this day nonblack ethnicities that have been and still are targets of discrimination, intolerance, and even genocide. The black community, consequently, does not have a monopoly on victimhood. Her overly simplistic and one-dimensional lens on history misses this fundamental fact. White Ukrainians, Poles, Kulaks, and Jews could educate her on what it means to be discriminated against for the particularities of personal appearance and culture. Whites are also not exclusively the perpetrators of this oppression. Black Africans enslaved other black Africans for centuries, from Ancient times, through the colonial era, and up to this day.[10] Historical obfuscation is a hallmark of ideological thinking and is due to a *deliberate* intellectual laziness among individuals and societies. As Voegelin's analyses point out, ideologists themselves engage in several psychological defense mechanisms, one of which includes the biased selective use of historical data to construct a one-dimensional and unilinear historical narrative extending from a remote past into the ideologue's present.[11] DiAngelo has fetishized the black/white dichotomy to such an extent that it is all she sees when observing social interactions, American culture, and world history. As a result, the vast complexity of historical phenomena is lost on her. She quite literally sees the world in "black and white."

What is more, Voegelin suggests a third avenue for commenting on DiAngelo's analysis of racism. One common trait of ideologies—from Bakunin and Marx to National Socialism and Fascism—is a logical trick which from the very start of an analysis of social, cultural, or political phenomena makes any and all critiques, questions, and contrary evidence which doesn't fully align with the ideological system further *confirmation* of the ideological analysis itself. In DiAngelo's case, her assertion that argumentation and "defensiveness" on the part of whites when she tells them they unwittingly perpetrate white privilege, fits squarely into this ideological mold. Her assertion makes a refutation of her thesis, or even attempts at refining it through an appeal to logic and evidence, merely an example of "white defensiveness" and "white fragility," and therefore proof that her thesis is correct. DiAngelo's brand of the Anti-Racist movement mendaciously conceals its true objective: not diversity but conformity, homogeneity cloaked as heterogeneity.[12]

Other internal incoherencies exist within DiAngelo's brand of the Anti-Racist movement that undermine its just aspirations. In what might be the most famous lines of the Civil Rights era, Martin Luther King famously declared, "I have a dream that my four little children will one day live in a nation where they will not be judged by the color of their skin but by the content of their character."[13] One of the essential points here is that the fight against racism entails an effort to assert the importance of individual identity over group identity. It is content of character that matters—that is, the unique personality—not the group-concept of "whiteness" or "blackness." Reifying these groups without perceiving the diversity within them perpetuates the same mode of thought responsible for racism in the first place.[14] Discrimination occurs because people assume that a person's race necessitates certain beliefs, actions, and behaviors. It engulfs the individual within the mass of group-identity, forgetting that the individual is unique and not necessarily defined by any particular determination of his/her physical appearance or background. As King and Voegelin remind us, the *individual* person is essential, not some nebulous group-concept that likely blurs or eclipses the actual diversity of characters within that group. The form that the Anti-Racist movement has taken today, as expressed in DiAngelo's work, is hard to distinguish from the mode of thought characteristic of what it was initially fighting against.

This toxic blend of apocalypticism and "identity politics" is not exclusive to the Anti-Racist Left. On January 6, 2021, a group of primarily white Donald Trump supporters fought past Capital police forces and stormed the U.S. Capital building in an overt attempt to foil the legal confirmation of Joe Biden's victory in the U.S. presidential election. Some of these individuals carried Confederate and Nazi-inspired paraphernalia, toted guns, and shouted surprisingly misinformed and senseless slogans. Despite all evidence to the contrary—the conservative majority Supreme Court's refusal to consider the case, bipartisan election observers, and no proof whatsoever that voter fraud took place on a scale that would affect the results—these men and women firmly believed the election was rigged against their candidate. No amount of evidence, logic, or appeals to good sense would persuade them. The "refusal to apperceive" reality, and thus have the capacity to discuss and communicate about it, is a basic feature of ideology. It makes communication impossible from the outset, with all parties stuck in a counterfeit reality of their own making.

Finally, it must be pointed out that one of the problematic trends seen in U.S. politics today is the belief that efforts to uphold standards of behavior on an individual, family, and societal level are in reality oppressive to those groups and individuals not sharing those same standards. "My president right or wrong," has become the phrase of the day. Disillusionment with the political process has transformed into blind loyalty to a politician's cult of personality, and this same politician has raised himself to a savior status. On the other side, the question "Who's to judge?" has become nauseatingly cliché, and it is often the Anti-Racist groups highlighted above who are most likely to ask it.[15] However, this line of reasoning only succeeds in undermining all basis for criticizing a racist viewpoint, since if all opinions and patterns of behavior are legitimized and in need of recognition, then the racist would also be entitled to his opinion and racist behavior, however much the antiracists abhor it. Taking the extreme view that Black and White "realities" are so incompatible as to preclude all communication between them suggests that the groups will forever be locked in a struggle to the death, with only one victor possible. White supremacists have their "reality," and the black community has theirs. The latter perceives the former as oppressive and in need of deconstruction; yet, *by their own admission*, the "reality" that would replace it would be just as repressive to nonblack groups. In the memorable lines of Herman Melville, we are left with a "Loose-Fish" in the violent abyss of the open ocean.

COMMUNICATION AND A COMMON REALITY?

As Voegelin's lifelong work demonstrates, political corruption, racism, and political messianism are great evils, and we must strive as individuals and societies to eradicate them to the extent that it is possible. However, the Anti-Racist left and the extreme Right have taken a unique approach. Instead of acknowledging that there might be room for debate about how to address societal issues, they engage in a transmuted form of *tribalism*—in essence, declaring that if one does not address an issue in *the specific way* they themselves imagine it should be, one is no less than an enemy who must be eradicated. This line of thought is exemplified in the words of Ibram Kendi: "One either allows racial inequities to persevere, as a racist, or confronts racial inequities, as an antiracist. There is no in-between safe space of 'not racist.' The claim of 'not racist' neutrality is a mask for racism."[16] For these Left and Right ideologues there exists *on principle* no compromise and no middle ground. If one suggests that addressing racial inequities is an extraordinarily complex and multidimensional problem, and that perhaps policies as simple as redistributing wealth or overthrowing essential institutions that have existed for centuries might not completely solve them, one becomes an ally of the enemy and a guardian of "white supremacy." If, on the other hand, one mentions that perhaps not all U.S. media outlets and business elites are part of some wide-ranging Leftist conspiracy to overthrow the white working class, one then turns into just another brainwashed conspirator. This type of "my way or the highway" approach to addressing real problems makes genuine dialogue about them impossible from the outset.

Yet, wherein lies the basis for communication then? How does one talk to, never mind convince, someone who believes substantive communication about real problems is nothing but pragmatic communication in disguise—or worse, white supremacy or Leftist conspiracy in disguise? Eric Voegelin's corpus makes this clear: we must appeal *not* to a common "experience," but to a common "reality" in which we all participate. Language—*the Logos*—is the key here, as it reflects this common reality and aims to express it. On a macrolevel, all cultures and societies have at least one thing in common: the attempt to endow the fact of their existence with *meaning* in terms of ends human and divine. Each in their own way, these societies establish relationships between Man, God, World, and Society.[17] On an individual level, we all seek answers to the mysteries of the "Beginning" and "Beyond" of our personal lives and struggle to come up with the language symbols that make these mysteries communicable. We live in complex societies, alongside other individuals with their unique struggles, interests, and purpose. But our *seeking to express, describe, and transmit these* elements is what roots us in common reality. For Voegelin, a common trait of all ideological systems is a denial of this shared reality of seeking in which all human beings "participate" to some degree. This denial cuts off one "reality" from another. It creates the conditions for the furtherance of racial, class, or gender separation, resulting inevitably in the mutual hatred of the respective parties. From each group's standpoint in this divide, the inability to communicate across its horizon is axiomatic.

Yet, as Voegelin shows, this common reality allows communication to exist in the first place. As a white man, I, of course, cannot "experience" the same thing a person of color experiences, in the same way I cannot share the experiences of any other human being on earth. However, for one to articulate this experience and another to be able to listen *sympathetically* to it, there must be some shared "something" in which we all participate. Otherwise, progress on racial justice issues in a predominantly white society would be hopeless. DiAngelo herself attests to this common reality when she describes how white people are supposed to react to the charge of racism. According to her, we are supposed to listen humbly when confronted with a racial misstep, acknowledge it, apologize for it, and seek to remedy it. *None of these steps would be possible without communication across racial divides.* The self-correction of our conscious and subconscious racial prejudices depends entirely on this common reality that Voegelin emphasizes.

To be sure, asserting the existence of a "common reality" does not mean there are not differing perspectives or that one group has a monopoly of truth on it. Disagreement about complex issues is inevitable. Nonetheless, if progress can be made in addressing them, all sides need at least to *assume* that logic, evidence, and fact still hold sway, and believe in the power of language. Moreover, solutions must be specific, not abstract, and we must keep in mind the hard-won historical insight that "final solutions" are a fable.

NOTES

1. For an interesting account of how the U.S. political system manages to renew itself repeatedly over the course of its history, see George Freedman, *The Storm before the Calm: America's Discord, the Crisis of the 2020s, and the Triumph Beyond* (New York: Random House, 2020).

2. Though I focus here on Robin DiAngelo's work, my critique applies equally to the work of Ibram Kendi. See Robin DiAngelo, *White Fragility: Why It's So Hard*

for White People to Talk about Racism (Boston: Beacon Press, 2018). Also, see Ibram Kendi, *How to Be an Anti-Racist* (New York: Random House, 2019).

3. Some of his earliest works were dedicated to this phenomenon. See Eric Voegelin, *Race and State* (Columbia: University of Missouri Press, 1997). Also, *The History of the Race Idea* (Columbia: University of Missouri Press, 1998).

4. For clarification, DiAngelo uses the term "ideology" in a way outside its original meaning and purpose. By the term, she means an unjustified and unjustifiable "world-view." For her, everyone has an "ideology." It is important that Voegelin criticizes this use of the term. An "Ideology" is not just any "opinion" on matters cultural, political, and historical. It has a very specific historical connotation, stemming from the work of the German Idealist School of Fichte, Kant, and Hegel, as well as their intellectual progeny in all Marxist, Fascist, and Postmodernist thought. DiAngelo's and Kendi's work is heavily influenced by these Marxist/Postmodernist elements. Whether or not they are aware of this influence is another question.

5. Voegelin actually suggests a third form of communication: intoxicating. For the purposes of this conclusion, though, I will focus on the first two. See Eric Voegelin, "Necessary Moral Bases for Communication in Democracy," in *The Eric Voegelin Reader: Politics, History, Consciousness*, ed. Charles Embry and Glenn Hughes (Columbia: University of Missouri Press 2017), 67.

6. DiAngelo, *White Fragility*, 41–42.

7. Hannah Arendt, *Responsibility and Judgment* (New York: Random House, 2003), 147.

8. For an analysis of how this historical obfuscation works, see Eric Voegelin, "On Hegel: A Study in Sorcery," in *Published Essays 1966–1985* (Columbia: University of Missouri Press, 1990).

9. Ibid.

10. See Giulio Meotti, "Slavery Rampant in Africa, Middle East; The West Wrongly Accuses Itself," The Gatestone Institute: International Policy Institute, July 5, 2020. https://www.gatestoneinstitute.org/16195/slavery-africa-middle-east.

11. Voegelin, "On Hegel: A Study in Sorcery."

12. This is a perfect illustration of what Allen Bloom calls the "Closing of the American Mind," (*The Closing of the American Mind: How Higher Education Has Failed Democracy and Impoverished the Souls of Today's Students* [New York: Simon and Schuster, 1987]).

13. Martin Luther King Jr., "I Have a Dream" (speech, March on Washington, Washington D.C, August 28, 1963). https://www.naacp.org/i-have-a-dream-speech-full-march-on-washington/.

14. Thomas Sowell, an African American economist and cultural critic, has argued persuasively that color is not necessarily a determinative factor in which "culture" one participates. See Thomas Sowell, *Black Rednecks and White Liberals* (New York: Encounter Books, 2006).

15. Kendi, *How to Be an Anti-Racist* (New York: Random House, 2019).

16. Eric Voegelin, *Order and History: Israel and Revelation* (Columbia: University of Missouri Press, 2001), 39–50.

17. Voegelin highlights the participatory complex of consciousness-reality-language. See Eric Voegelin, *Order and History: In Search of Order* (Columbia: University of Missouri Press, 2000), 31–33.

Bibliography

Altizer, Thomas J. "A New History and a New But Ancient God? Voegelin's The Ecumenic Age." In *Eric Voegelin's Thought: A Critical Appraisal*, ed. Ellis Sandoz, 184. Durham: Duke University Press, 1982.

Arendt, Hannah. *Responsibility and Judgment*. New York: Random House, 2003.

Bergson, Henri. *The Creative Mind: An Introduction to Metaphysics*. Mineola: Dover Publications, 2007.

Bloom, Allen. *The Closing of the American Mind: How Higher Education Has Failed Democracy and Impoverished the Souls of Today's Students*. New York: Simon and Schuster, 1987.

Cameron, Averil. "Remaking the Past." In *Interpreting Late Antiquity: Essays on the Postclassical World*, ed. G. W. Bowersock, Peter Brown, and Oleg Grabar, 1–20. Cambridge: Belknap Press of Harvard University Press, 2001.

Congar, Yves. *The Meaning of Tradition*. Tr. A. N. Woodrow. San Francisco: Ignatius Press, 2004.

Cooper, Barry. *The End of History: An Essay on Modern Hegelianism*. Toronto: University of Toronto Press, 1984.

———. *Eric Voegelin and the Foundations of Modern Political Science*. Columbia: University of Missouri Press, 1999.

Corrington, John. "Order and Consciousness/Consciousness and History: The New Program of Voegelin." in *Eric Voegelin's Search for Order in History*, ed. Stephen A. McKnight.

Dale, Eric Michael. *Hegel, the End of History, and the Future*. Cambridge: Cambridge University Press, 2014.

DiAngelo, Robin. *White Fragility: Why It's So Hard for White People to Talk about Racism*. Boston: Beacon Press, 2018.

Drury, Shadia B. *Alexandre Kojève: The Roots of Postmodern Politics*. New York: St. Martin's Press, 1994.

Federici, Michael. *Eric Voegelin: The Restoration of Order*. Wilmington: ISI books, 2002.

Ferrarin, Alfredo. *Hegel and Aristotle*. New York: Cambridge University Press, 2001.

Fowden, Garth. "Varieties of Religious Community." In *Interpreting Late Antiquity: Essays on the Postclassical World*, ed. G. W. Bowersock, Peter Brown, and Oleg Grabar, 82–106. Cambridge: Belknap Press of Harvard University Press, 2001.

Fukuyama, Francis. *The End of History and the Last Man*. New York: Free Press, 2006.

———. *Identity: The Demand for Dignity and the Politics of Resentment*. New York: Farrar, Strauss, and Giroux, 2018.

Gouin, Jean-Luc. "Der Instinkt Der Vernünftigkeit: De L'Inaliénabilité de la Rationalité." In *Hegel-Studien*, Band 44, January 29, 2010.

Grier, Philip T. "The End of History and the Return of History." In *The Hegel Myths and Legends*, ed. Jon Stewart. Evanston: Northwestern University Press, 1996.

Hegel, Georg Wilhelm Friedrich. *Elements of the Philosophy of Right*. Ed. Allen Wood. Tr. H. B. Nisbet. New York: Cambridge University Press, 1991.

———. *Lectures on the Philosophy of History*. Tr. J Sibree. New York: Dover Publications, 1956.

———. *Lectures on the Philosophy of Religion: The Lectures of 1827*. Ed. Peter Hodgson. Tr. R. F. Brown, P. C. Hodgson, and J. M. Stewart. New York: Oxford University Press, 2007.

———. *The Phenomenology of Spirit*. Tr. A. V. Miller. New York: Oxford University Press, 1977.

———. *The Science of Logic*. Tr. A. V. Miller. Amherst: Humanity Books, 1969.

Herndon, Jeffrey. *Eric Voegelin and the Problem of Christian Political Order*. Columbia: University of Missouri Press, 2007.

Hughes, Glenn. *Transcendence and History*. Columbia: University of Missouri Press, 2003.

Huntington, Samuel. *The Clash of Civilizations and the Remaking of World Order*. New York: Touchstone, 1996.

Husserl, Edmund. *Crisis of the European Sciences and Transcendental Phenomenology*. Evanston: Northwestern University Press, 1970.

Kendi, Ibram. *How to Be an Anti-Racist*. New York: Random House, 2019.

Kojève, Alexandre. *Introduction à la lecture de Hegel*. Ed. Raymond Queneau. Mesnil-sur-l'Estrée: Gallimard, 2001.

Laing, R. D. *The Divided Self: An Existential Study in Sanity and Madness*. Kindle Ebook Edition.

Lenin, Vladimir. "Imperialism, the Highest Stage of Capitalism." In *The Lenin Anthology*, ed. and tr. Robert C. Tucker. New York: W. W. Norton and Company, 1975.

Lipset, Seymour Martin. *Political Man*. New York: Doubleday, 1960.

Lonergan, Bernard. *Insight*. Toronto: University of Toronto Press, 1992.

Löwith, Karl. *From Hegel to Nietzsche: The Revolution in 19th Century Thought*. New York: Anchor Books, 1967.

———. *Meaning in History: The Theological Implications of the Philosophy of History*. Chicago: University of Chicago Press, 1957.

Malabou, Catherine. *L'avenir de Hegel*. Paris: J. Vrin, 1996.

Magee, Glenn Alexander. *Hegel and the Hermetic Tradition.* Ithaca: Cornell University Press, 2001.

McMahon, Robert. "Eric Voegelin's Paradoxes of Consciousness and Participation." *The Review of Politics* Vol. 61, no. 1 (Winter, 1999): 117–139.

Mearsheimer, John. *The Tragedy of Great Power Politics.* New York: Norton Paper Backs, 2001.

Nichols, James H. *Alexandre Kojève: Wisdom at the End of History.* Lanham: Rowman and Littlefield Publishers, 2007.

O'Regan, Cyril. *The Heterodox Hegel.* Albany: State University of New York Press, 1994.

Pinkard, Terry. *Hegel: A Biography.* New York: Cambridge University Press, 2000.

Raeder, Linda C. "Voegelin on Gnosticism, Modernity, and the Balance of Consciousness." In *VoegelinView*, March 2020.

Rebillard, Eric. *Christians and Their Many Identities in Late Antiquity: North Africa, 200–450 CE.* Ithaca: Cornell University Press, 2012.

Sokolowski, Robert. *Introduction to Phenomenology.* New York: Cambridge University Press, 2000.

Sowell, Thomas. *Black Rednecks and White Liberals.* New York: Encounter Books, 2006.

Voegelin, Eric. *Anamnesis.* Columbia: University of Missouri Press, 1990.

———. "Configurations of History." In *Published Essays: 1966–1985*, 95. Columbia: University of Missouri Press, 1990.

———. *From Enlightenment to Revolution.* Durham: Duke University Press, 1975.

———. "Necessary Moral Bases for Communication in Democracy." In *The Eric Voegelin Reader: Politics, History, Consciousness*, ed. Charles Embry and Glenn Hughes. Columbia: University of Missouri Press, 2017.

———. "On Hegel: A Study in Sorcery." In *Published Essays: 1966–1985*, 213. Columbia: University of Missouri Press, 1990.

———. *Order and History Volume 1: Israel and Revelation.* Columbia: University of Missouri Press, 2001.

———. *Order and History Volume 2: The World of the Polis.* Columbia: University of Missouri Press, 2000.

———. *Order and History Volume 3: Plato and Aristotle.* Columbia: University of Missouri Press,

———. *Order and History Volume 4: The Ecumenic Age.* Columbia: University of Missouri Press, 2000.

———. *Order and History Volume 5: In Search of Order.* Columbia: University of Missouri Press,

———. "Response to Professor Altizer's 'A New History and a New But Ancient God?'" In *Published Essays: 1966–1985*, 292. Columbia: University of Missouri Press, 1990.

———. *Selected Correspondence: 1950–1984.* Columbia: University of Missouri Press, 2007.

————. "What Is History?" In *What Is History? and Other Late Unpublished Writings*, ed. Thomas Hollweck and Paul Caringella, 1. Columbia: University of Missouri Press, 1990.

Von Doderer, Heimito. *The Demons*. Alfred A. Knopf, 1961.

Ziehen, Peter. *Disunited Nations*. New York: HarperCollins, 2020.

Zizek, Slavoj. *Less Than Nothing: Hegel and the Shadow of Dialectical Materialism*. New York: Verso Books, 2012.

————. *Living in the End Times*. New York: Verso Books, 2010.

Index

About the Author

Michael J. Colebrook completed his doctorate of philosophy at the University of Dallas, where he defended his dissertation in 2015 on Eric Voegelin's Critique of the End of History Thesis. His research has focused primarily on political philosophy, philosophy of education, and international relations theory.

Michael has held a number of teaching positions at the university level, including at the University of Dallas and Assumption University. He taught Bioethics, Morality and Justice, and French for seven years at St. John's High School in Shrewsbury, Massachusetts, and is now the headmaster at Tulsa Classical Academy in Tulsa, Oklahoma.

His writings appear in journals such as the *International Journal of Christianity and Education*, *The Strategy Bridge*, and *VoegelinView*. In addition to his academic and professional career in education, Michael also serves as an intelligence officer in the United States Army Reserves, and has performed the duties of company commander, operations officer, platoon leader, and counterintelligence section lead.

In his free time, Michael enjoys reading, writing, gardening, hiking, Crossfit, and spending time with his family. He and his wife, Michele, have been married for nine years and have three beautiful children.

www.ingramcontent.com/pod-product-compliance
Lightning Source LLC
Chambersburg PA
CBHW031134270326
41929CB00011B/1627